FIRST 50 FOLK SONGS
YOU SHOULD PLAY ON THE PIANO

ISBN 978-1-4950-9563-4

Hal • Leonard®

7777 W. Bluemound Rd. P.O. Box 13819 Milwaukee, WI 53213

In Australia Contact:
Hal Leonard Australia Pty. Ltd.
4 Lentara Court
Cheltenham, Victoria, 3192 Australia
Email: ausadmin@halleonard.com.au

Visit Hal Leonard Online at
www.halleonard.com

AMAZING GRACE

Words by JOHN NEWTON
Traditional American Melody

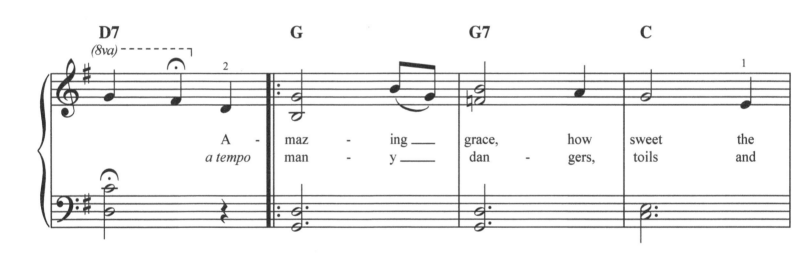

A - maz - ing ___ grace, how sweet the
man - y ___ dan - gers, toils and

sound that saved a ___ wretch like me! ___
snares I have al - read - y come. ___

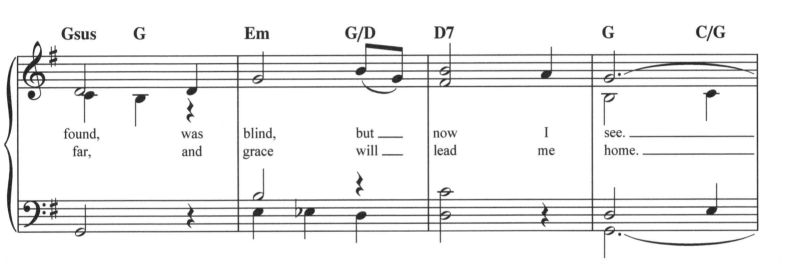

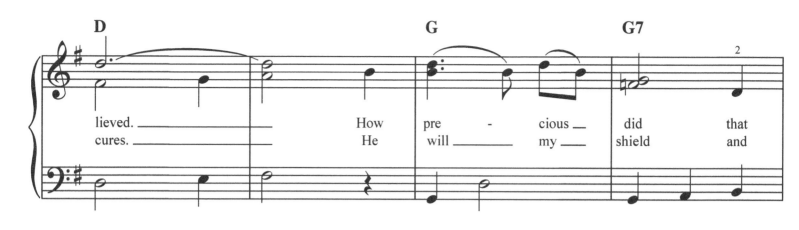

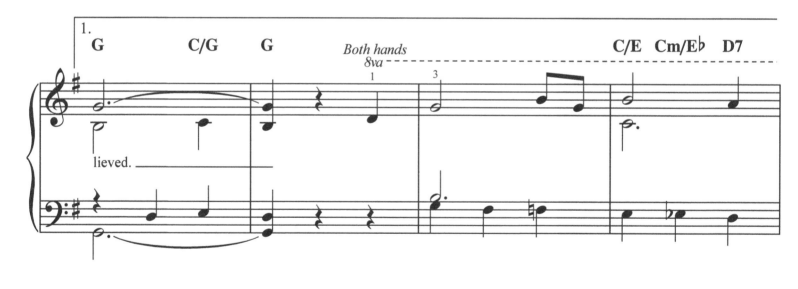

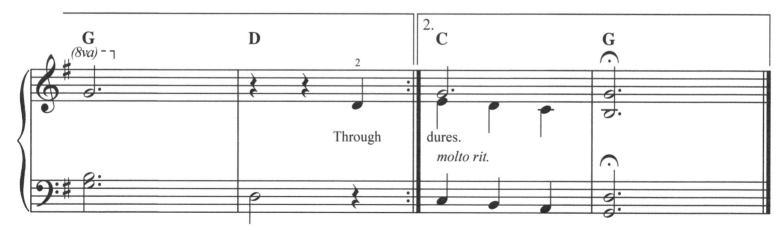

BARBARA ALLEN

Traditional English

In Scar - let - town where I was born there was a fair maid dwell - in', made ev - 'ry youth cry ___ "Well - a - day!" Her name was Bar - b'ra Al - len.

ARKANSAS TRAVELER

Southern American Folksong

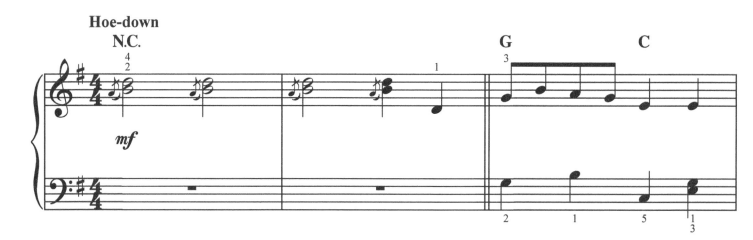

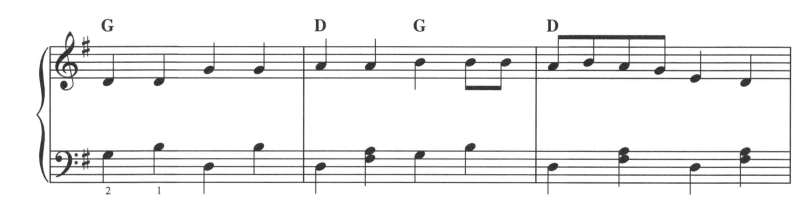

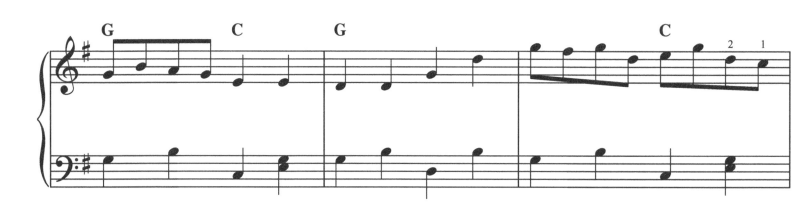

BEAUTIFUL BROWN EYES

Traditional

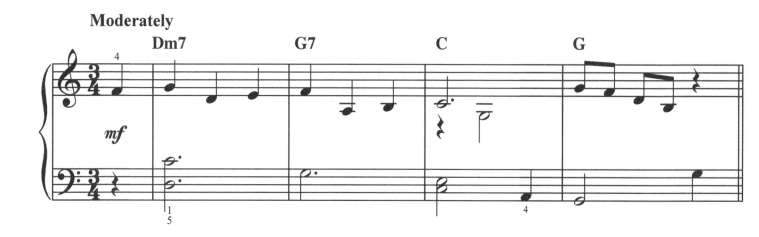

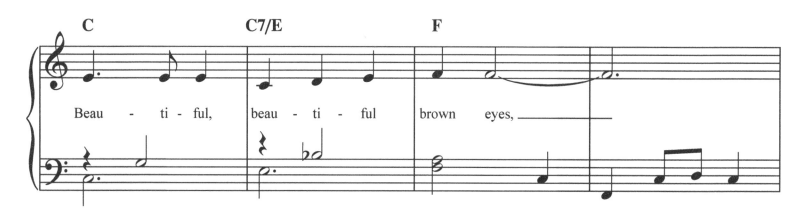

Beau - ti - ful, beau - ti - ful brown eyes, ____

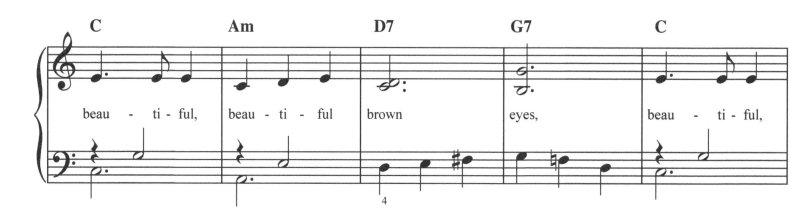

beau - ti - ful, beau - ti - ful brown eyes, beau - ti - ful,

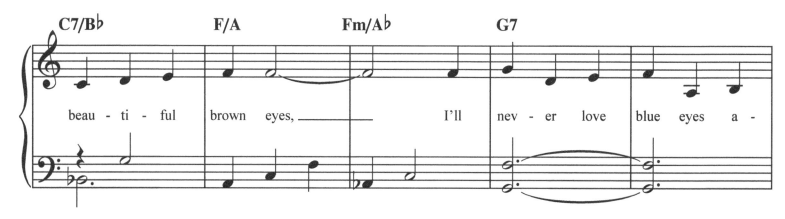

beau - ti - ful brown eyes, ____ I'll nev - er love blue eyes a -

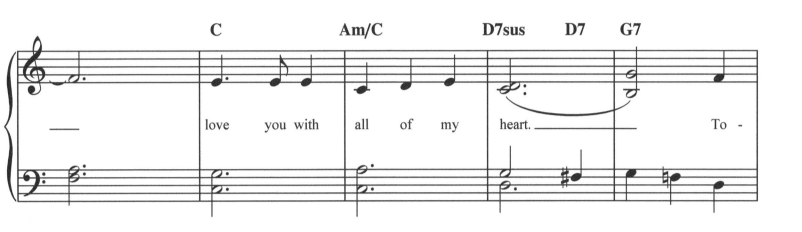

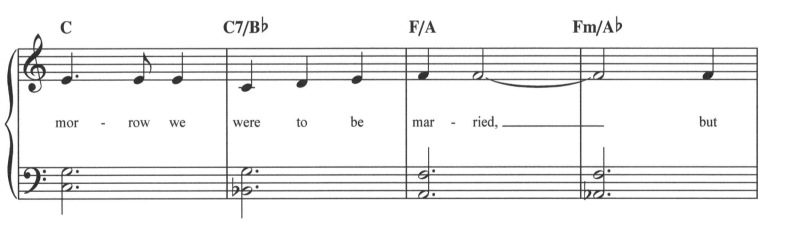

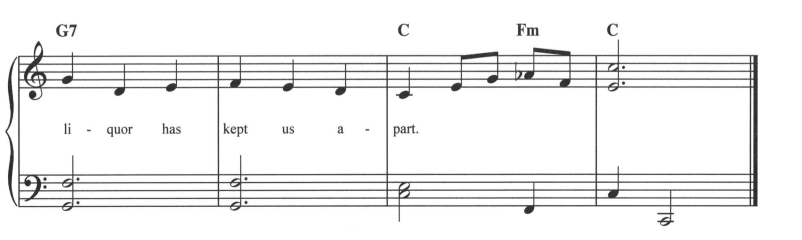

BUFFALO GALS
(Won't You Come Out Tonight?)

Words and Music by
COOL WHITE (JOHN HODGES)

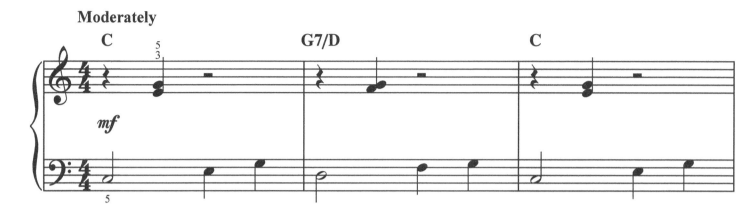

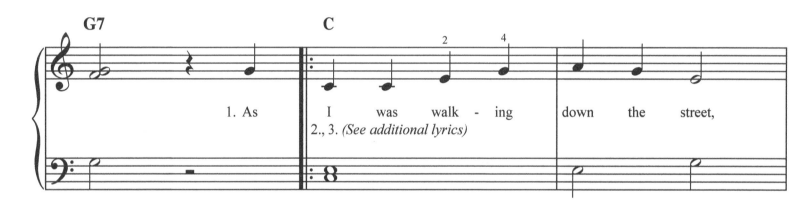

1. As I was walk-ing down the street,
2., 3. *(See additional lyrics)*

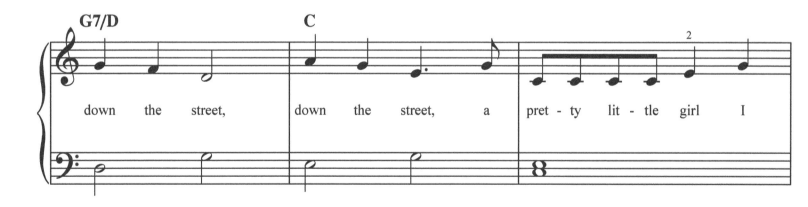

down the street, down the street, a pret-ty lit-tle girl I

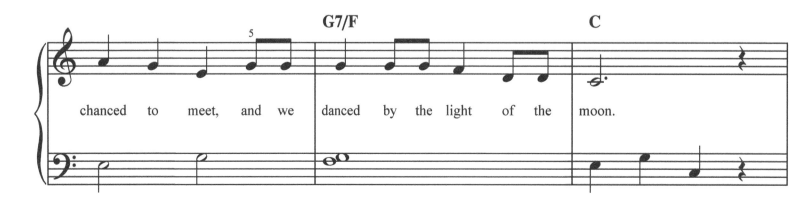

chanced to meet, and we danced by the light of the moon.

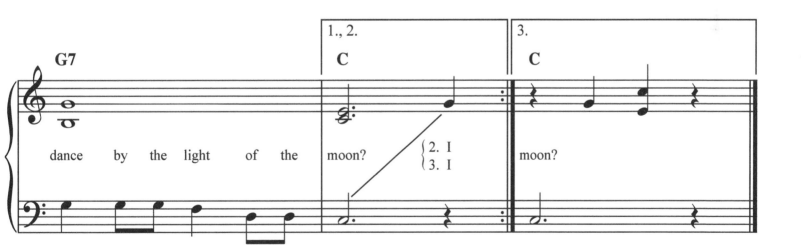

Additional Lyrics

2. I asked her if she'd stop and talk, stop and talk, stop and talk,
Her feet took up the whole sidewalk, and left no room for me.
Chorus

3. I asked her if she'd be my wife, be my wife, be my wife,
Then I'd be happy all my life, if she'd marry me.
Chorus

BURY ME NOT ON THE LONE PRAIRIE

Words based on the poem "The Ocean Burial"
by REV. EDWIN H. CHAPIN
Music by OSSIAN N. DODGE

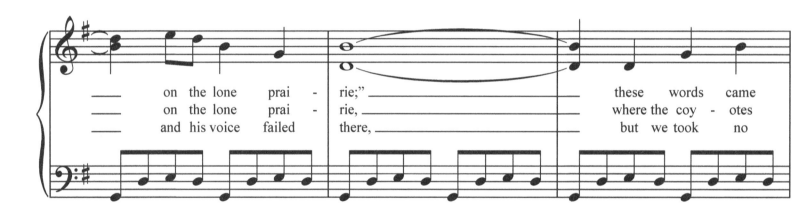

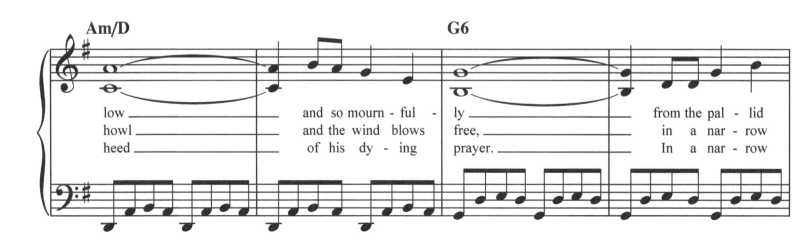

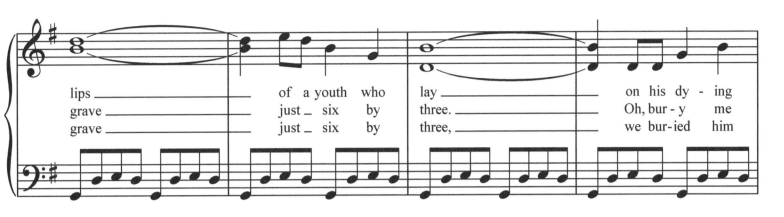

lips _____ of a youth who lay _____ on his dy - ing
grave _____ just _ six by three. _____ Oh, bur - y me
grave _____ just _ six by three, _____ we bur - ied him

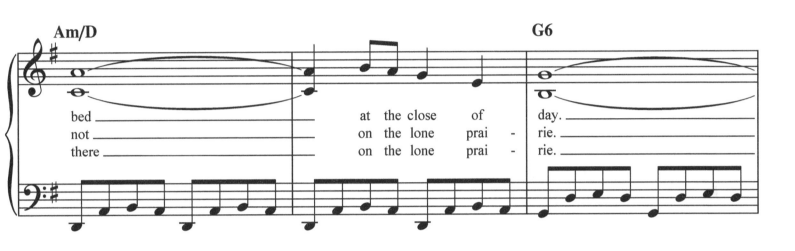

Am/D   **G6**

bed _____ at the close of day. _____
not _____ on the lone prai - rie. _____
there _____ on the lone prai - rie. _____

1., 2.   **3.**

N.C.   **N.C.**   **C6**

_____ "Oh, bur - y me ____ Yes, we bur - ied him there _____
_____ Oh, bur - y me

                                                        Dm

_____ on the lone prai - rie, _____ where the owl all night _____

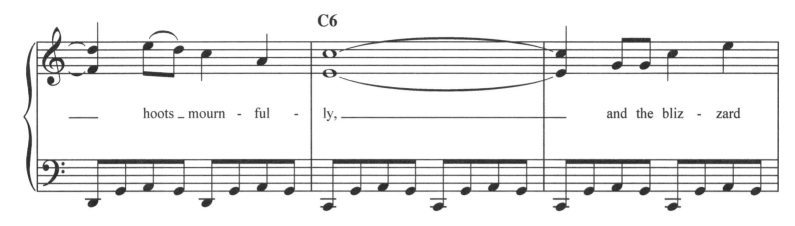

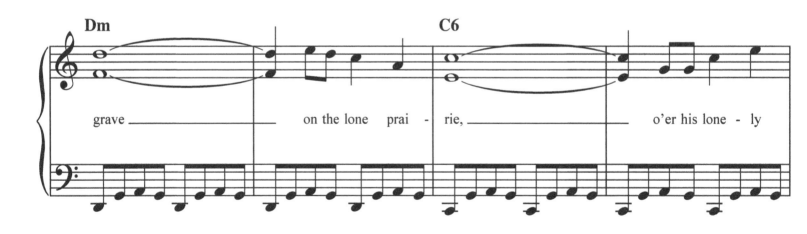

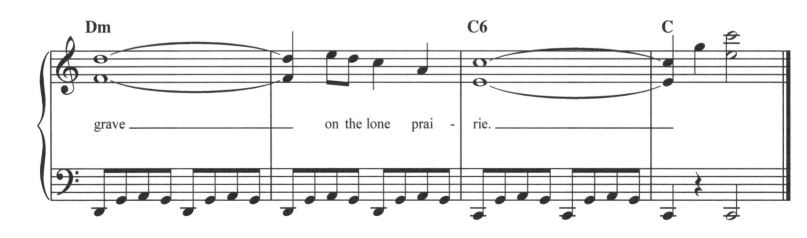

CORRINA

Traditional

Moderately slow

Cor - ri - na, Cor - ri - na, ___ where'd you stay last night?
ri - na ___ a - cross ___ the sea.

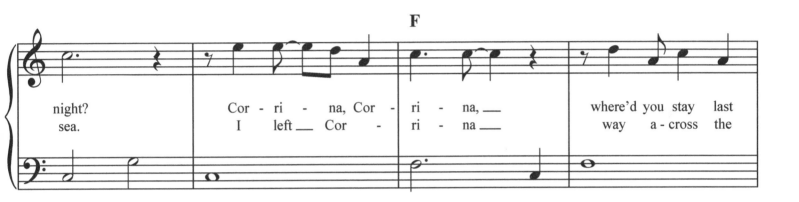

Cor - ri - na, Cor - ri - na, ___ where'd you stay last night?
I left ___ Cor - ri - na ___ way a - cross the sea.

Come in ___ this morn - in', ___ sun was shin - in' bright. ___
She won't write me no let - ter, ___ she don't care ___ for me. ___

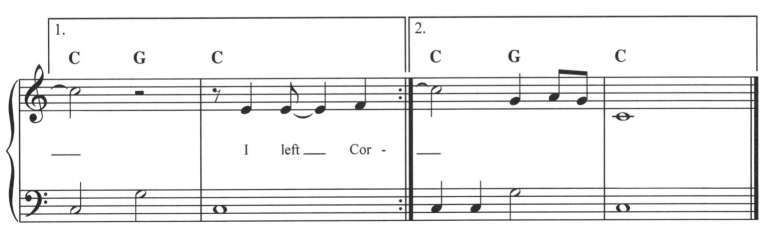

1.
C   G   C
___ I left ___ Cor -

2.
C   G   C

CINDY

Southern Appalachian Folksong

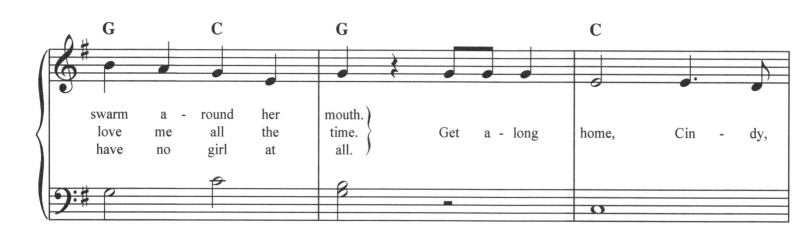

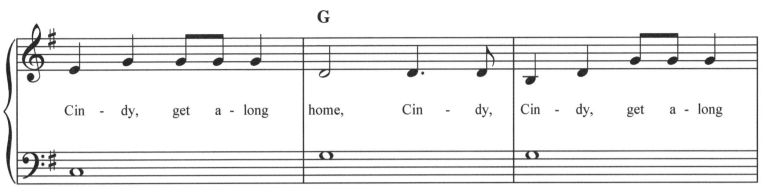

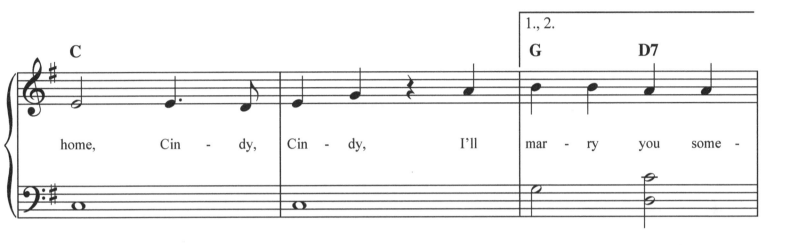

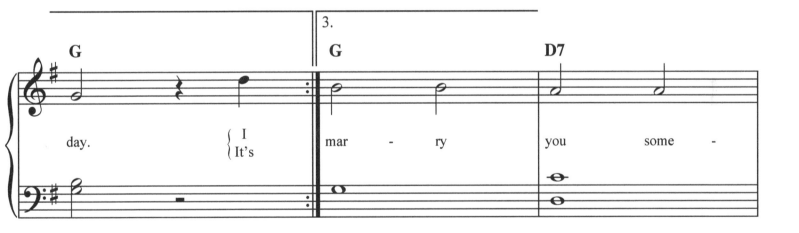

THE CRAWDAD SONG

Traditional

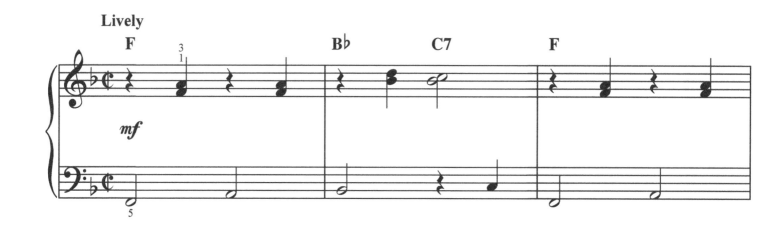

You get a line and I'll get a pole, my

hon - ey. _____ You get a line and

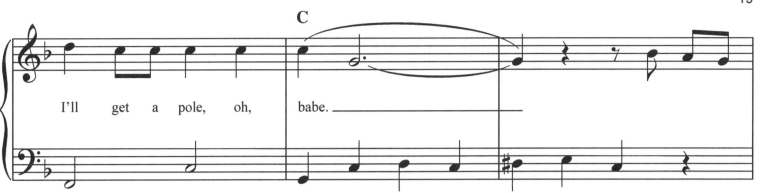

I'll get a pole, oh, babe.

You get a line and I'll get a pole,

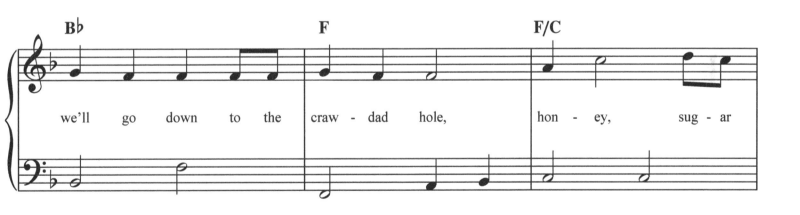

we'll go down to the craw - dad hole, hon - ey, sug - ar

ba - by mine!

DOWN BY THE RIVERSIDE

African-American Spiritual

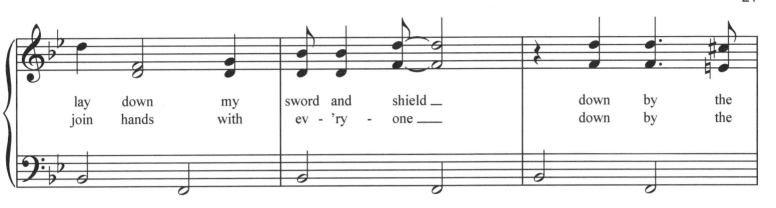

lay down my sword and shield __ down by the
join hands my with ev - 'ry - one __ down by the

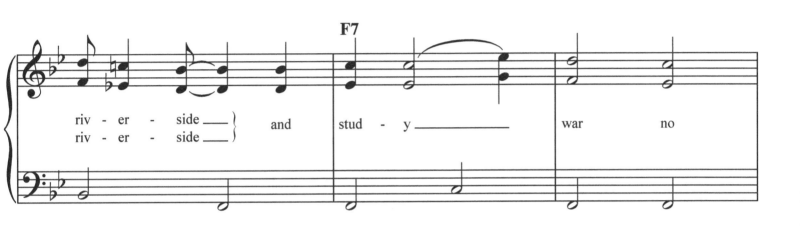

F7

riv - er - side __ and stud - y _____ war no
riv - er - side __

Bb

1. 2. **Bb7**

more. Gon - na I ain't gon - na

Eb **Bb**

stud - y war no more, __ I ain't gon - na stud - y war no more, __

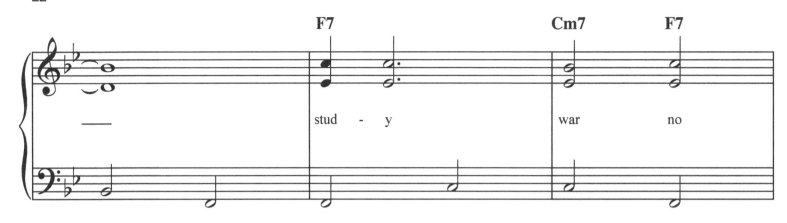

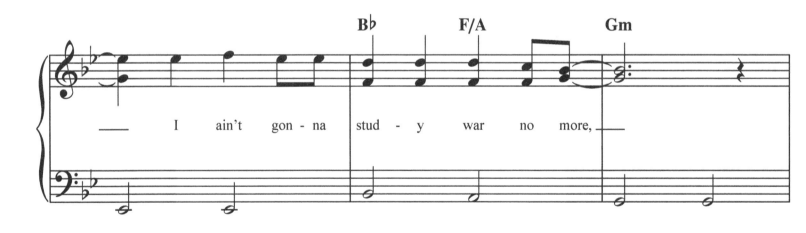

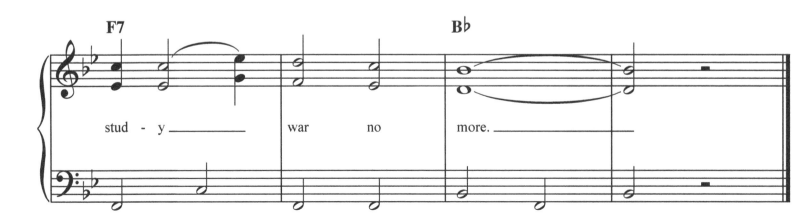

(I Wish I Was In)
DIXIE

Words and Music by
DANIEL DECATUR EMMETT

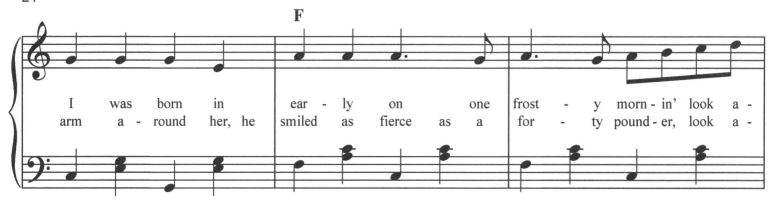

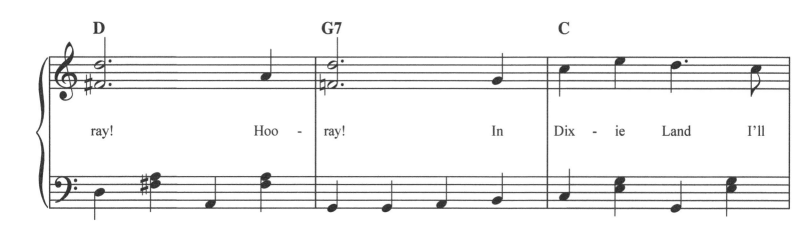

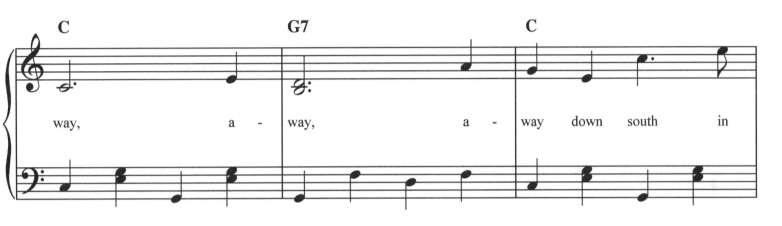

DOWN IN THE VALLEY

Traditional American Folksong

Down in the val -
sun -
let -

ley,
shine,
ter,

val - ley so
vi - 'lets love
send it by

low, ___
dew, ___
mail; ___

late in the
an - gels in
send it in

eve -
heav -
care

ning
en
of

hear the train
know I love
Birm - ing - ham

FREIGHT TRAIN

Words and Music by
ELIZABETH COTTEN

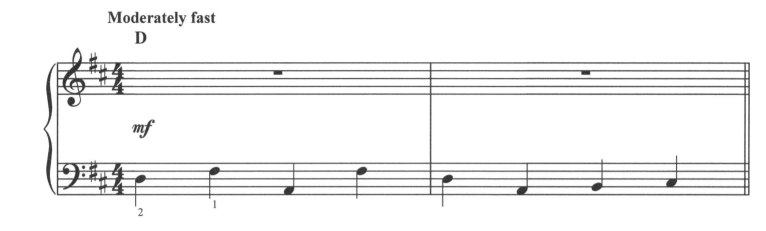

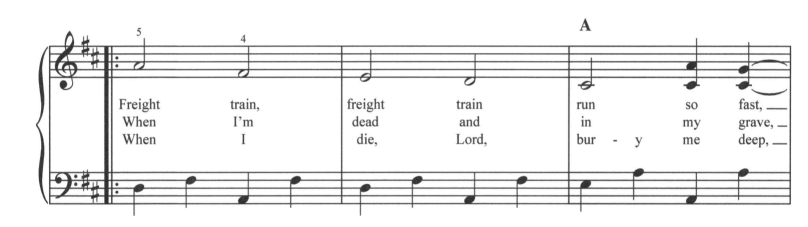

Freight   train,   freight   train   run   so   fast, __
When I'm   dead   and   in   my   grave, __
When I   die,   Lord,   bur - y me   deep, __

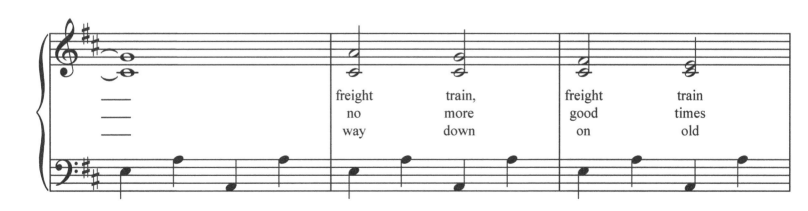

__   freight   train,   freight   train
__   no   more   good   times
__   way   down   on   old

GOOD NIGHT LADIES

Words by E.P. CHRISTY
Traditional Music

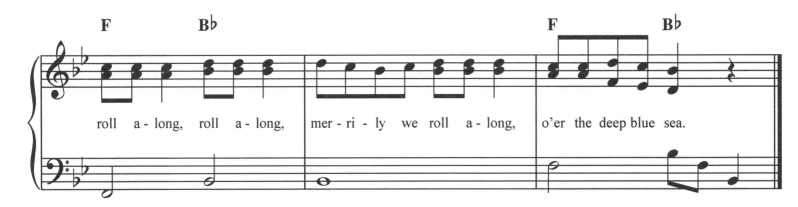

HESITATION BLUES

Words and Music by BILLY SMYTHE
and J. SCOTT MIDDLETON

Moderately

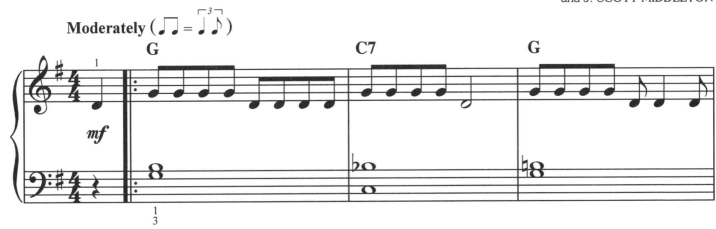

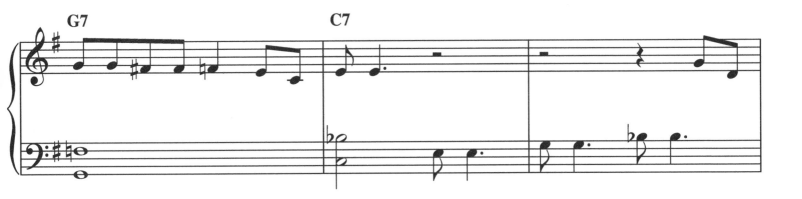

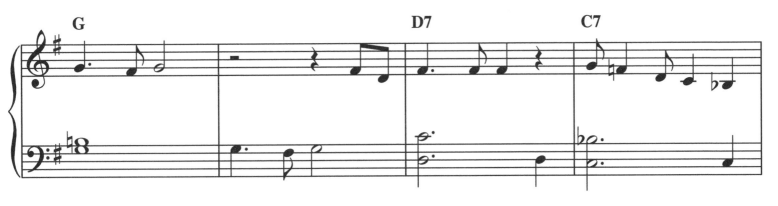

HOME ON THE RANGE

Lyrics by DR. BREWSTER HIGLEY
Music by DAN KELLY

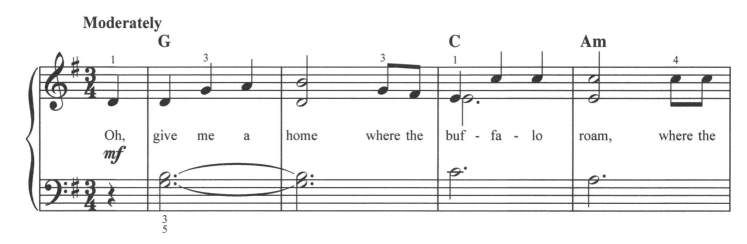

Oh, give me a home where the buf - fa - lo roam, where the

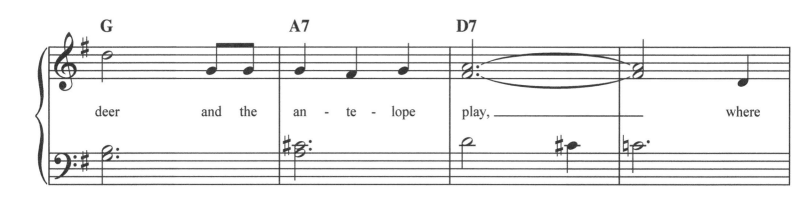

deer and the an - te - lope play, _____ where

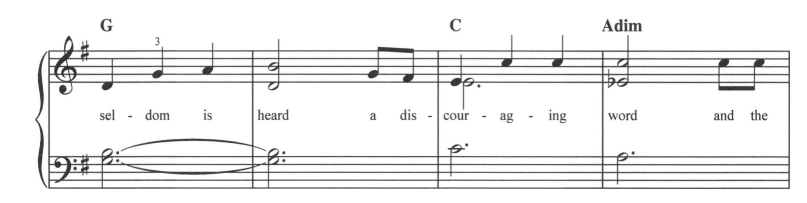

sel - dom is heard a dis - cour - ag - ing word and the

skies are not cloud - y all day.

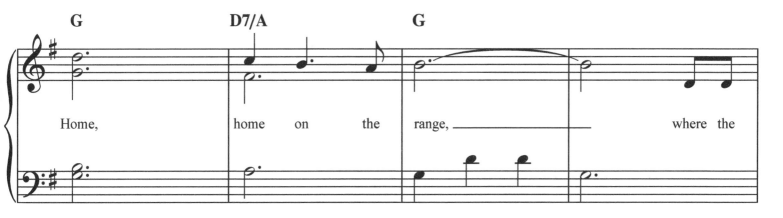

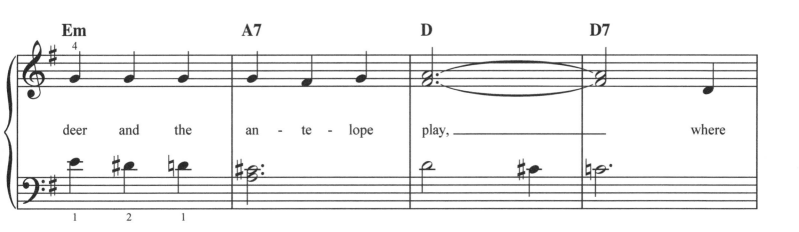

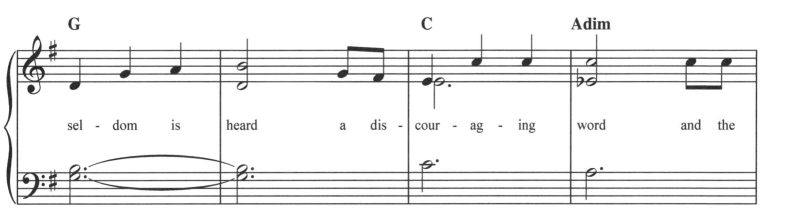

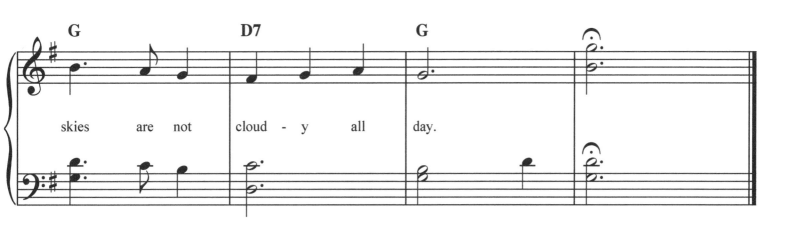

I'VE BEEN WORKING ON THE RAILROAD

American Folksong

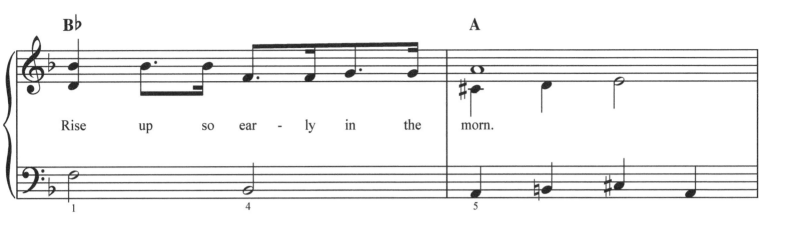

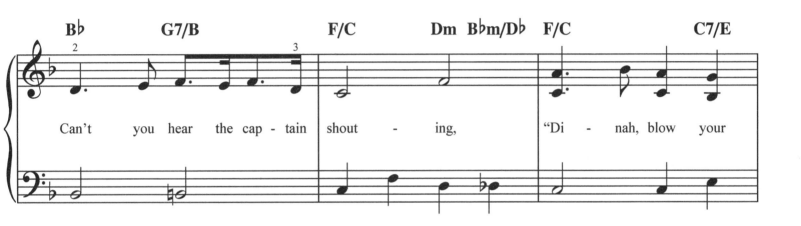

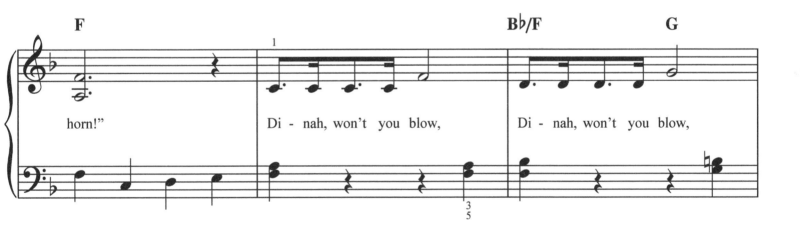

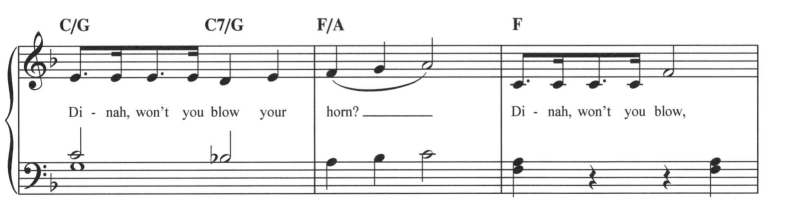

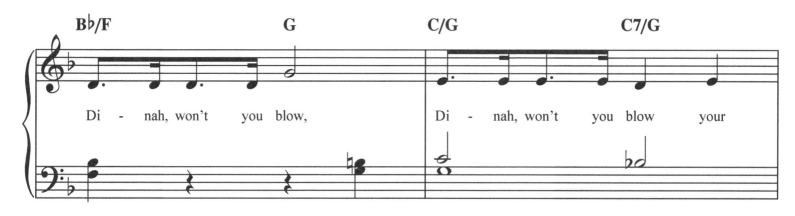

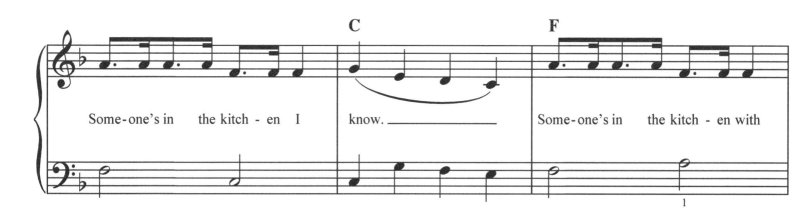

"Fee, fi, fid - dle - ee - i - o, fee, fi, fid - dle - ee - i -

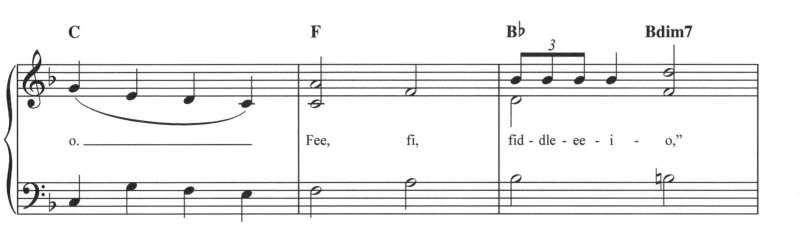

C **F** **B♭** **Bdim7**

o. _____ Fee, fi, fid - dle - ee - i - o,"

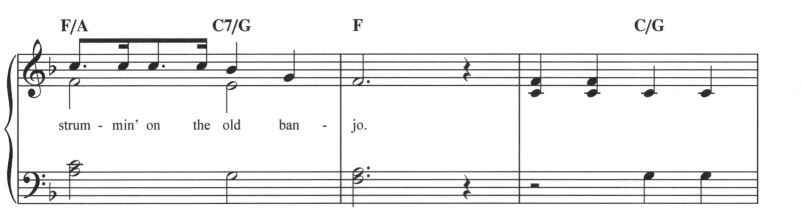

F/A **C7/G** **F** **C/G**

strum - min' on the old ban - jo.

G/D **C/G** **C** **G/B** **C7/B♭** **F**

IN THE GOOD OLD SUMMERTIME

Words by REN SHIELDS
Music by GEORGE EVANS

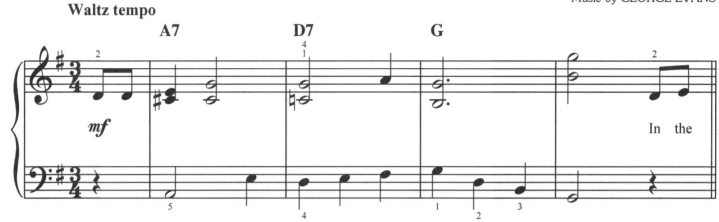

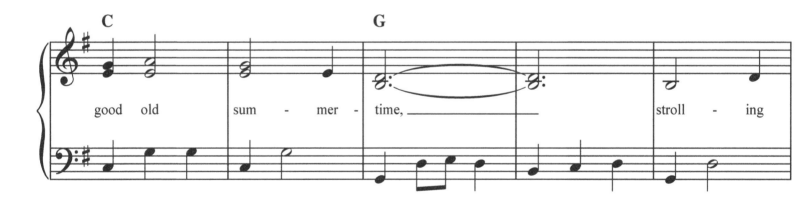

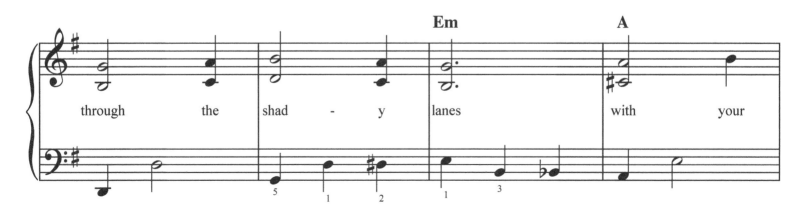

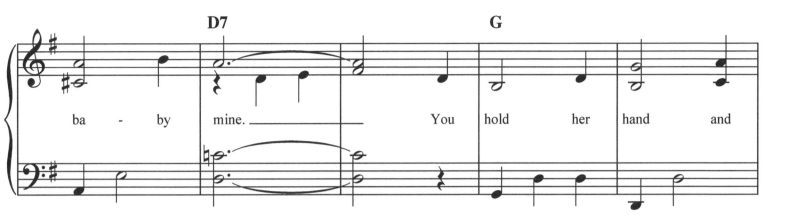

ba - by mine. _____ You hold her hand and

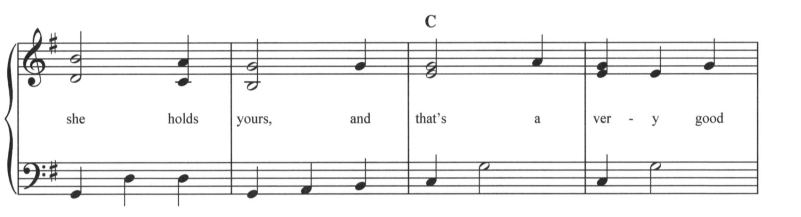

she holds yours, and that's a ver - y good

sign _____ that she's your toot - sey woot - sey

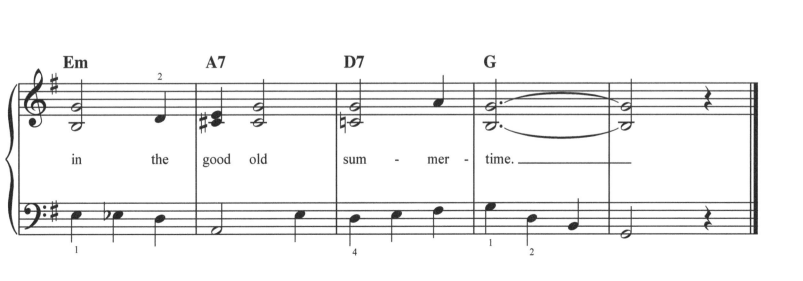

in the good old sum - mer - time. _____

JOHN BROWN'S BODY

Traditional

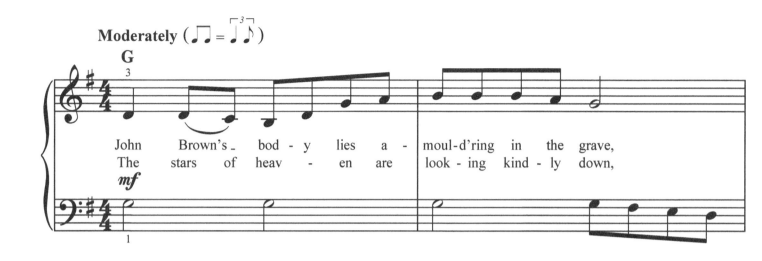

John Brown's bod-y lies a- moul-d'ring in the grave,
The stars of heav-en are look-ing kind-ly down,

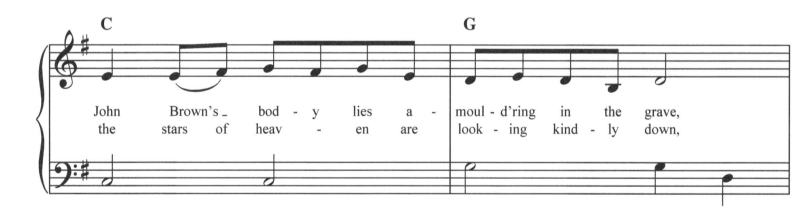

John Brown's bod-y lies a- moul-d'ring in the grave,
the stars of heav-en are look-ing kind-ly down,

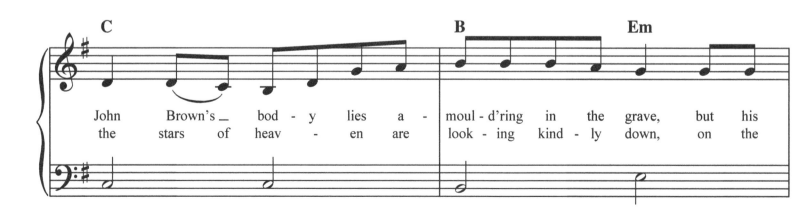

John Brown's bod-y lies a- moul-d'ring in the grave, but his
the stars of heav-en are look-ing kind-ly down, on the

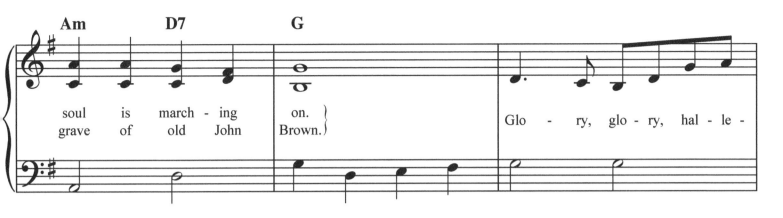

soul   is   march - ing   on.   Glo - ry, glo - ry, hal - le -
grave   of   old   John   Brown.

lu - jah!   Glo - ry, glo - ry, hal - le - lu - jah!

Glo - ry, glo - ry, hal - le - lu - jah! His

soul   is   march - ing   on.   on.

JOHN HENRY

West Virginia Folksong

Moderate Folk-Blues

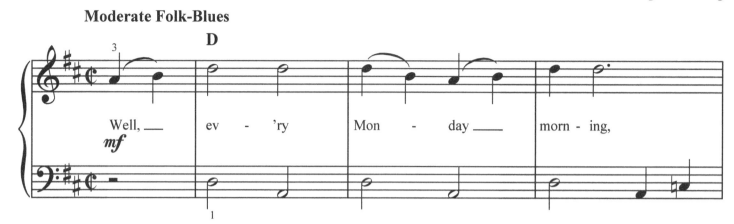

Well, ___ ev - 'ry Mon - day ___ morn - ing,

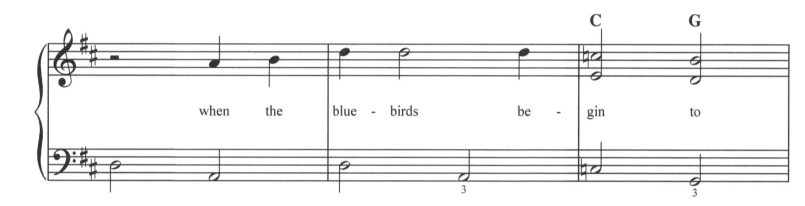

when the blue - birds be - gin to

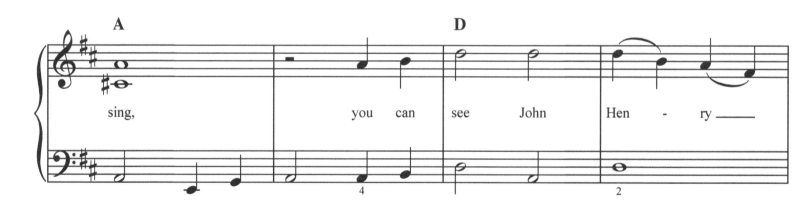

sing, you can see John Hen - ry ___

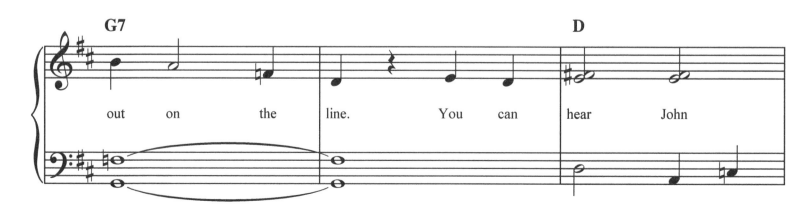

out on the line. You can hear John

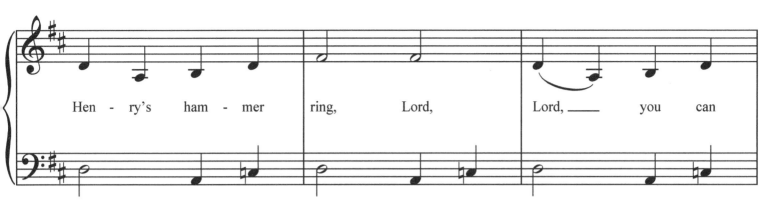

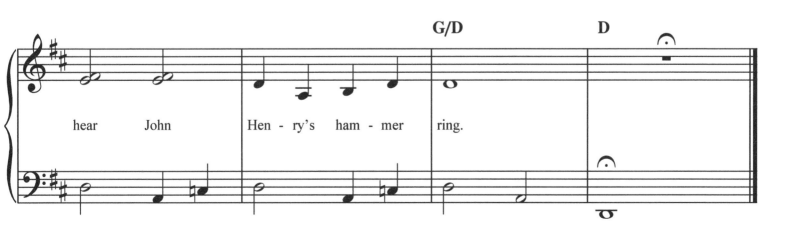

KUMBAYA

Congo Folksong

Slowly, like a hymn

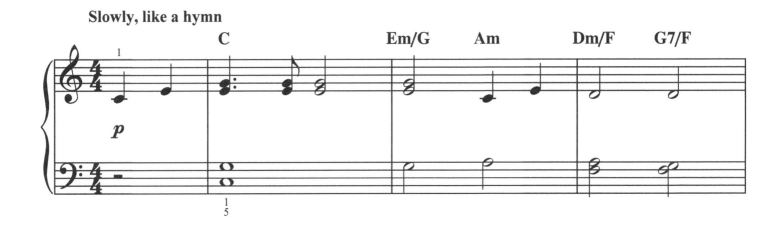

Kum - ba - ya, my Lord, kum - ba -
cry - ing, Lord, kum - ba -
pray - ing, Lord, kum - ba -
need you, Lord, kum - ba -

ya! Kum - ba - ya, my Lord, kum - ba -
ya! Hear me cry - ing, Lord, kum - ba -
ya! Hear me pray - ing, Lord, kum - ba -
ya! Oh, I need you, Lord, kum - ba -

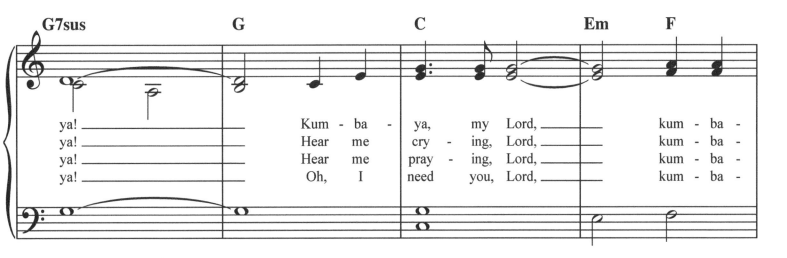

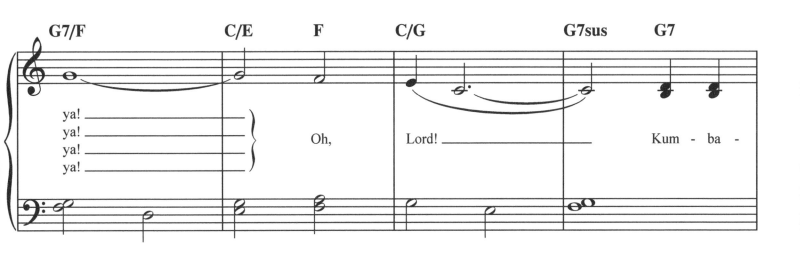

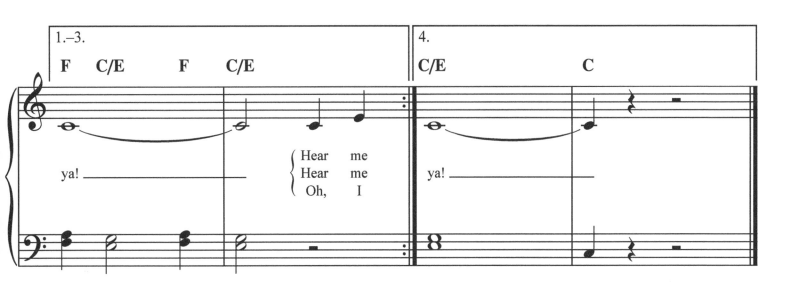

LITTLE BROWN JUG

Words and Music by
JOSEPH E. WINNER

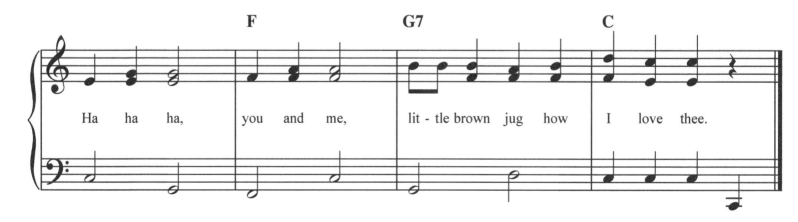

MAKE ME A PALLET ON THE FLOOR

Traditional

MAN OF CONSTANT SORROW

Traditional

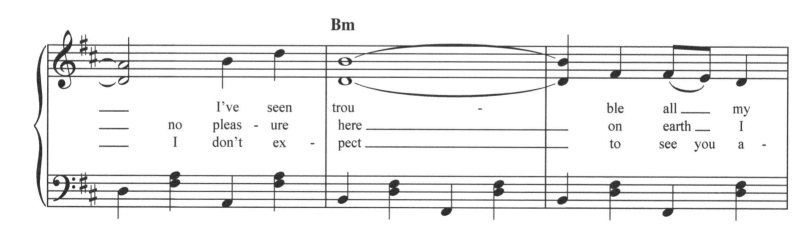

MATTY GROVES

English Folksong

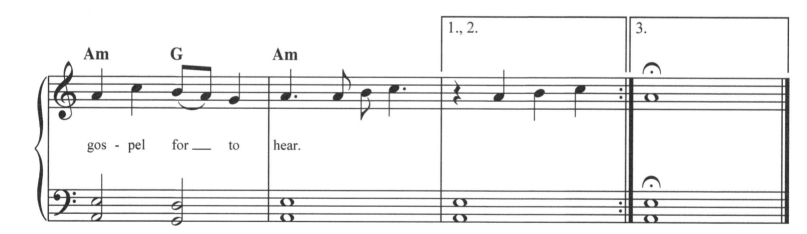

Additional Lyrics

2. And when the meeting, it was done, she cast her eyes about,
   And there she saw little Matty Groves walking in the crowd.

3. Come home with me, little Matty Groves, come home with me tonight.
   Come home with me, little Matty Groves, and sleep with me till light.

MIDNIGHT SPECIAL

Railroad Song

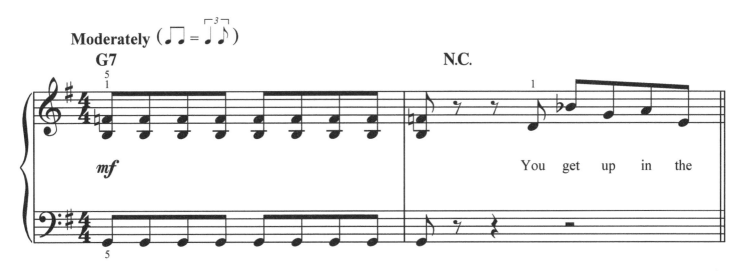

morn - in', ____ you hear the ding - dong
Hous - ton, ____ you'd bet - ter walk on
Lu - cy, ____ how in the world do you

ring. Now you look up - on a ta - ble, ____
by. Oh, you bet - ter not ___ gam - ble, boy,
know? I know by her a - pron ___

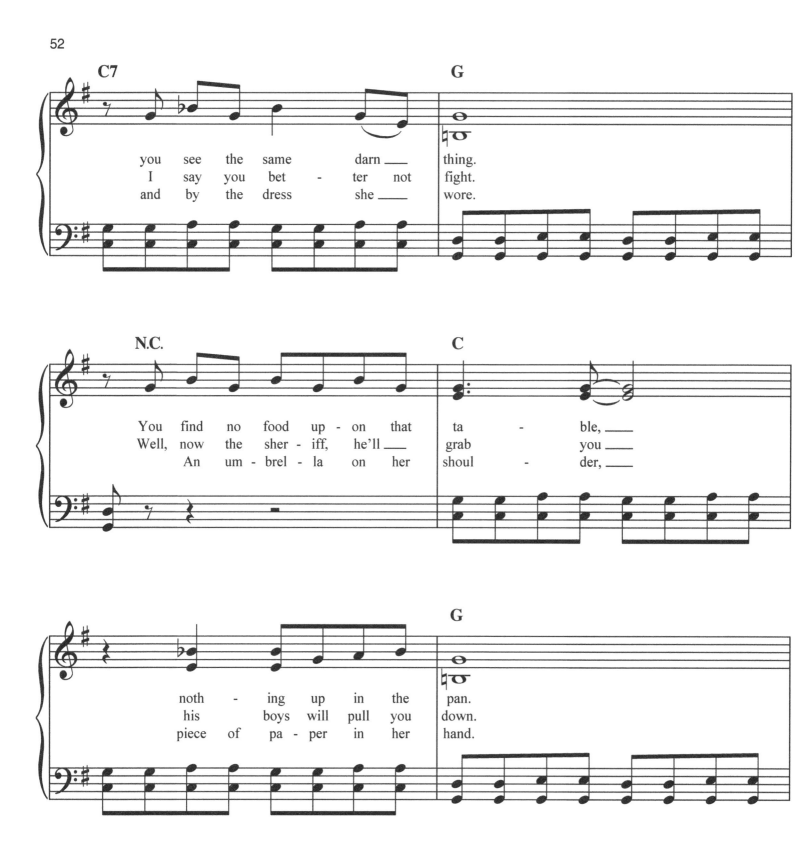

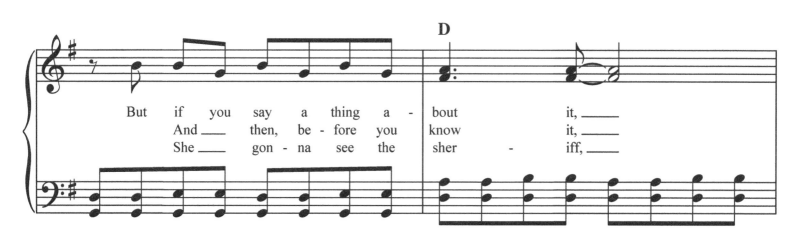

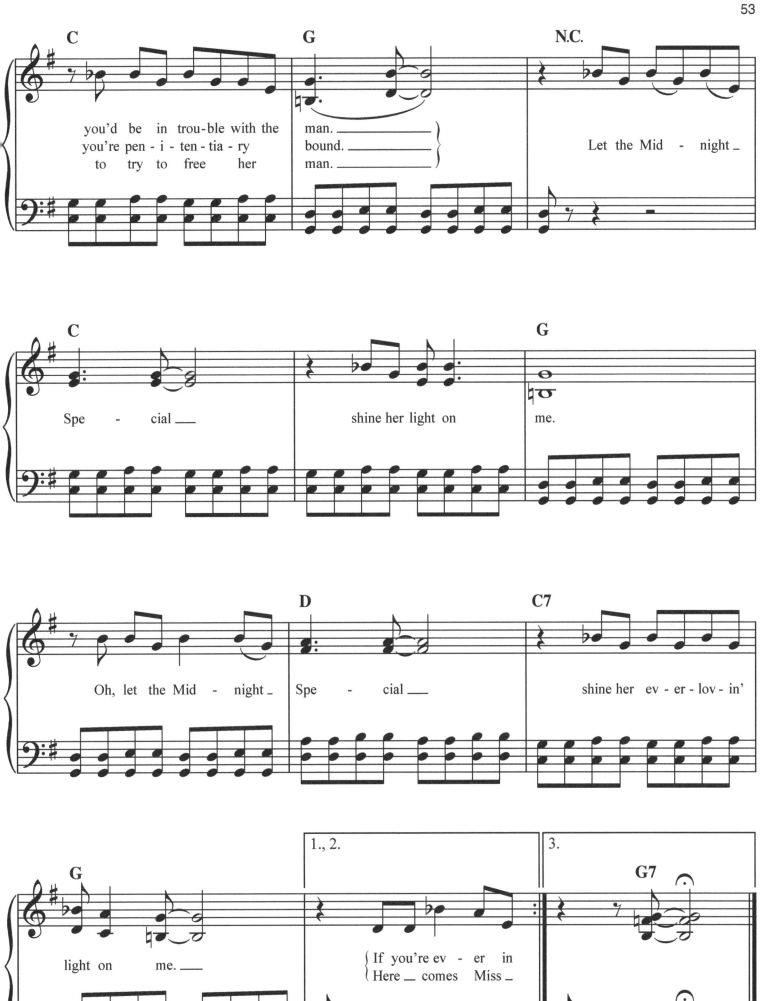

MICHAEL ROW THE BOAT ASHORE

Traditional Folksong

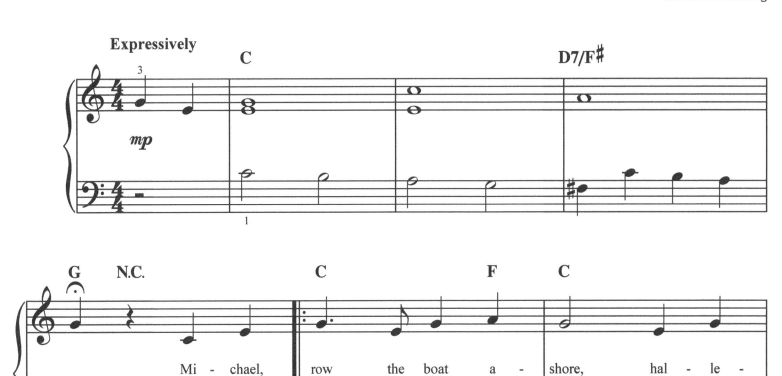

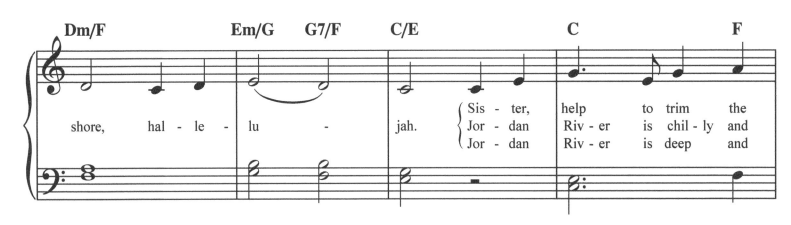

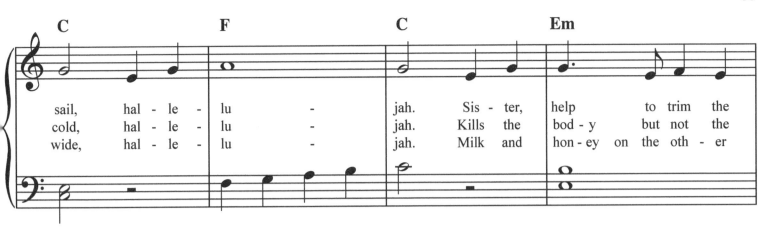

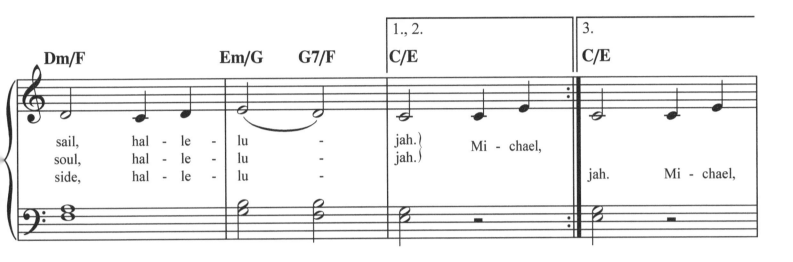

MY OLD KENTUCKY HOME

Words and Music by
STEPHEN C. FOSTER

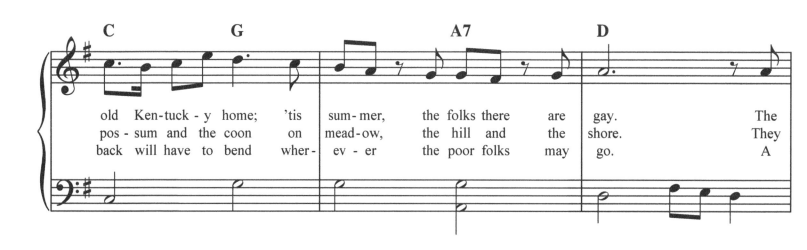

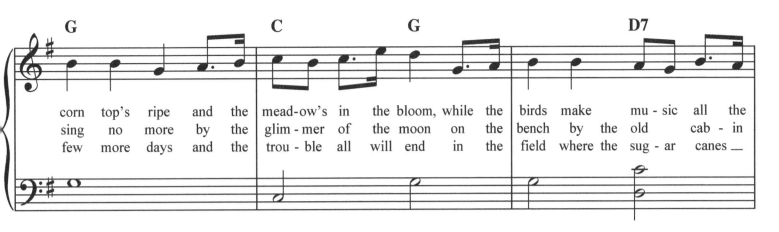

corn top's ripe and the | mead-ow's in the bloom, while the | birds make mu - sic all the
sing no more by the | glim - mer of the moon on the | bench by the old cab - in
few more days and the | trou - ble all will end in the | field where the sug - ar canes __

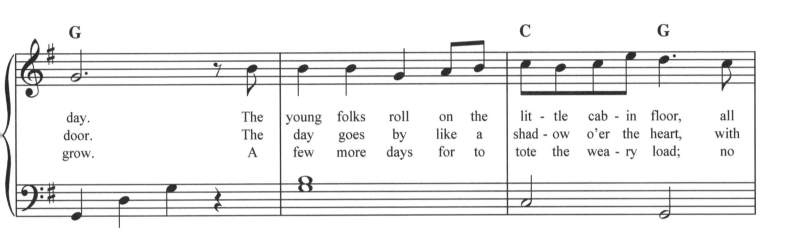

day. The | young folks roll on the | lit - tle cab - in floor, all
door. The | day goes by like a | shad - ow o'er the heart, with
grow. A | few more days for to | tote the wea - ry load; no

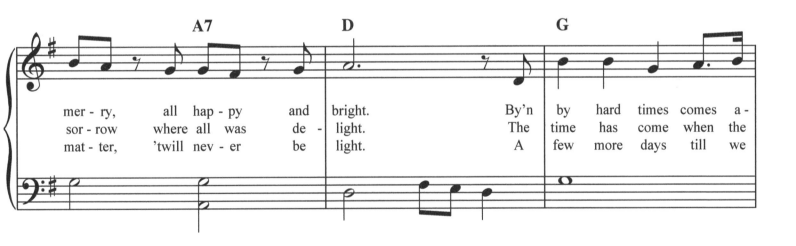

mer - ry, all hap - py and | bright. By'n by hard times comes a-
sor - row where all was de - | light. The time has come when the
mat - ter, 'twill nev - er be | light. A few more days till we

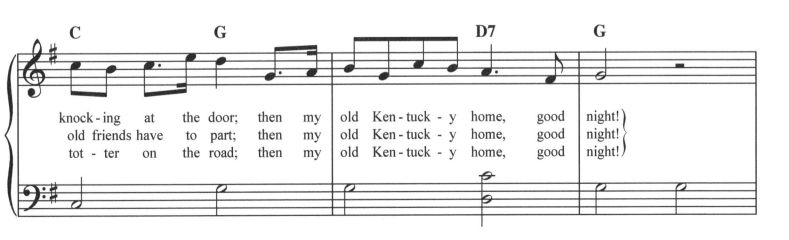

knock - ing at the door; then my | old Ken - tuck - y home, good | night!)
old friends have to part; then my | old Ken - tuck - y home, good | night!)
tot - ter on the road; then my | old Ken - tuck - y home, good | night!)

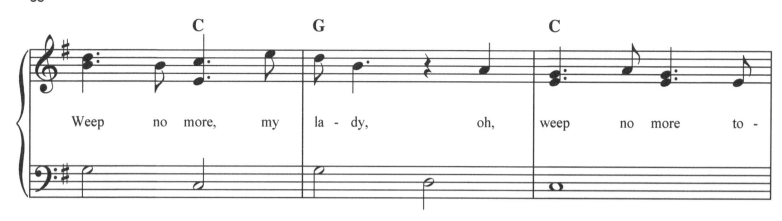

Weep no more, my la - dy, oh, weep no more to -

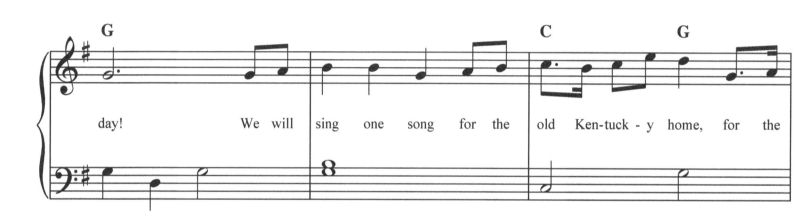

day! We will sing one song for the old Ken-tuck - y home, for the

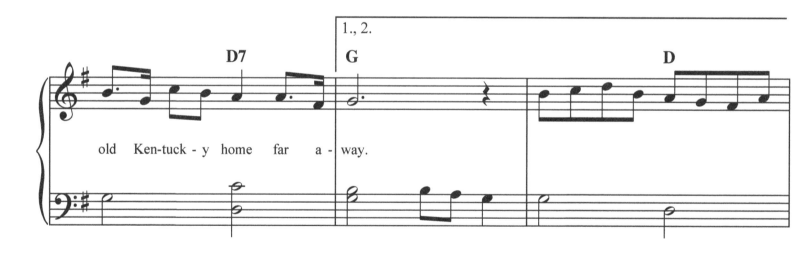

1., 2.

old Ken-tuck - y home far a - way.

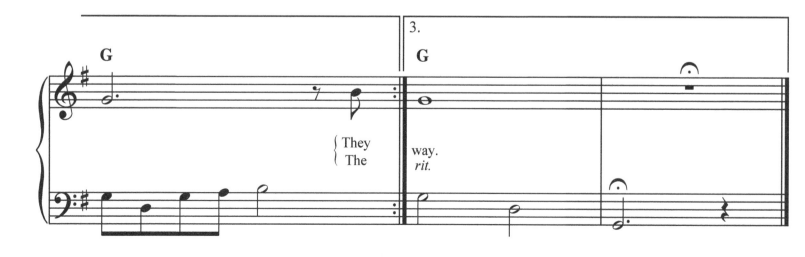

3.

They
The

way.
rit.

SHE'LL BE COMIN' 'ROUND THE MOUNTAIN

Traditional

NOBODY KNOWS THE TROUBLE I'VE SEEN

African-American Spiritual

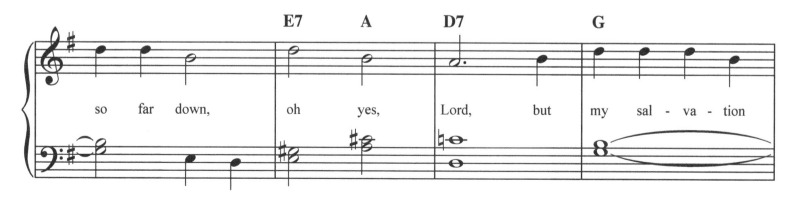

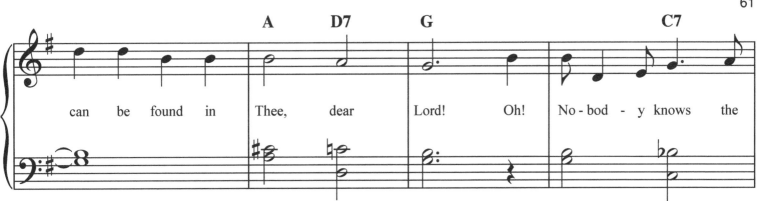

can be found in Thee, dear Lord! Oh! No-bod-y knows the

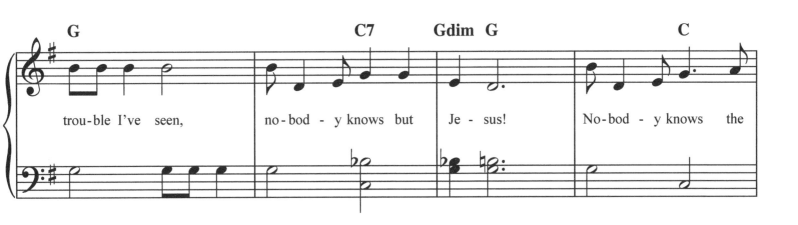

trou-ble I've seen, no-bod-y knows but Je-sus! No-bod-y knows the

trou-ble I've seen, glo-ry hal-le-lu-jah!

OH! SUSANNA

Words and Music by
STEPHEN C. FOSTER

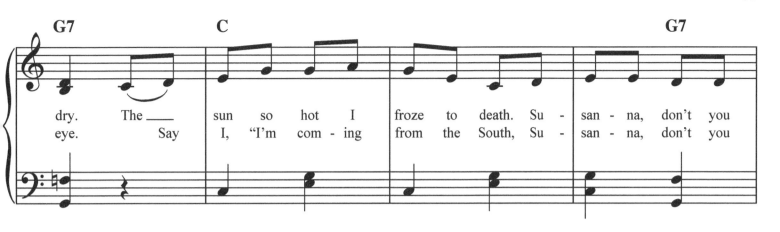

OLD FOLKS AT HOME
(Swanee River)

Words and Music by
STEPHEN C. FOSTER

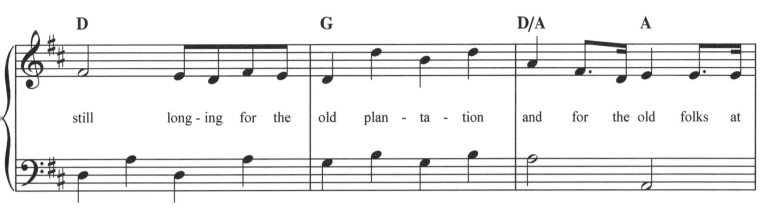

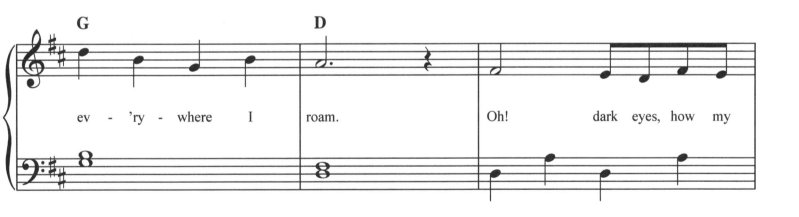

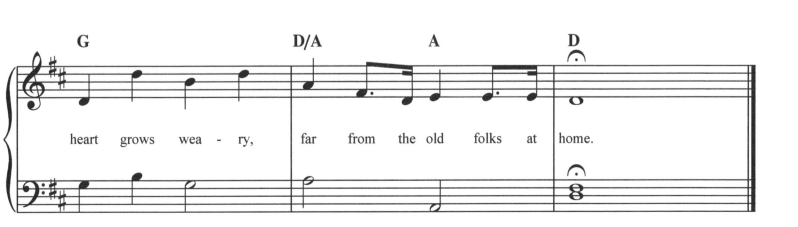

THE RED RIVER VALLEY

Traditional American Cowboy Song

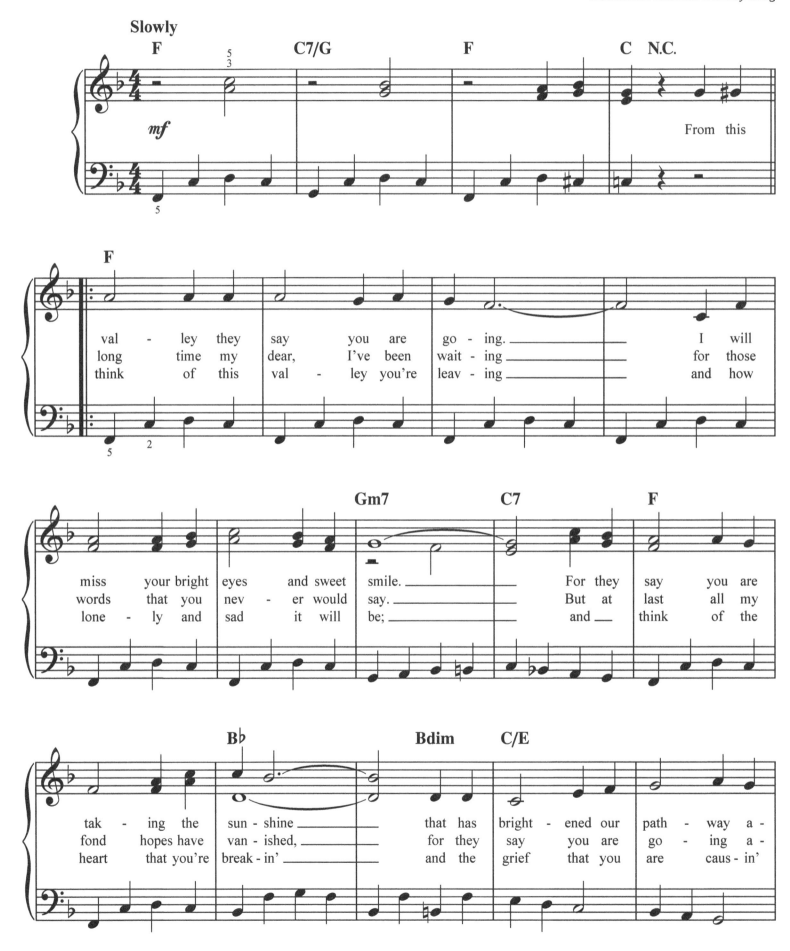

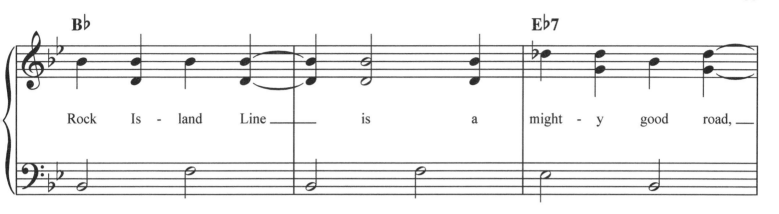

Bb   **Eb7**

Rock Is - land Line _____ is   a   might - y good road, ___

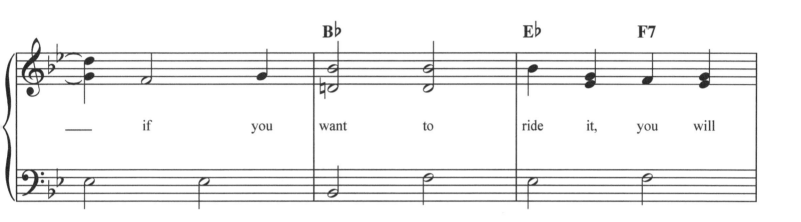

Bb   **Eb**   **F7**

___ if   you   want   to   ride it, you will

Bb   **Eb**   **F7**   **Bb**

go   like   you're   a -   fly - in'. Buy   your   tick - et   at   the

Eb   **F7**   **Bb**

sta - tion   on   the   Rock   Is -   land   Line.

SCARBOROUGH FAIR

Traditional English

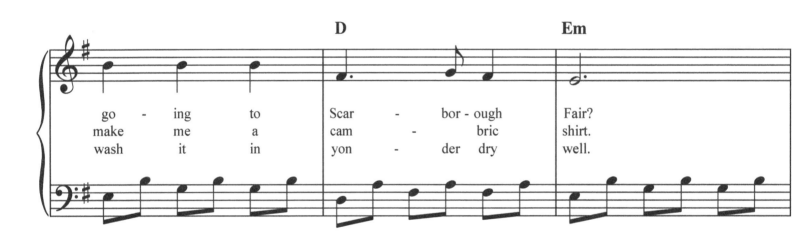

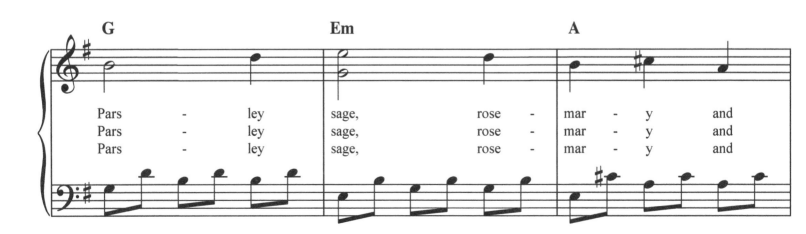

SHE WORE A YELLOW RIBBON

Words and Music by
GEORGE A. NORTON

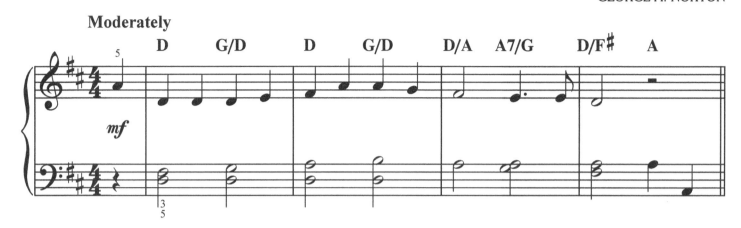

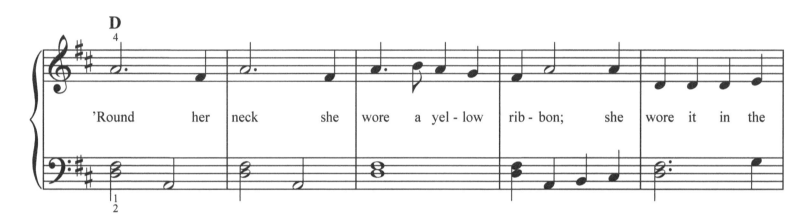

'Round her neck she wore a yel-low rib-bon; she wore it in the

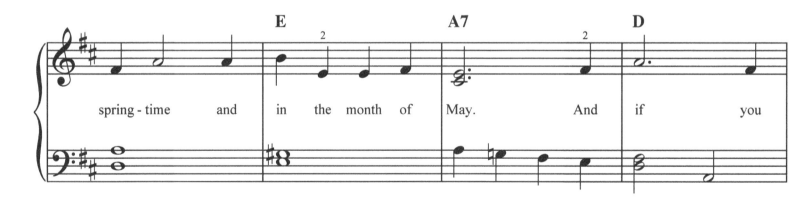

spring-time and in the month of May. And if you

asked her why the heck she wore it, she says, "It's for my

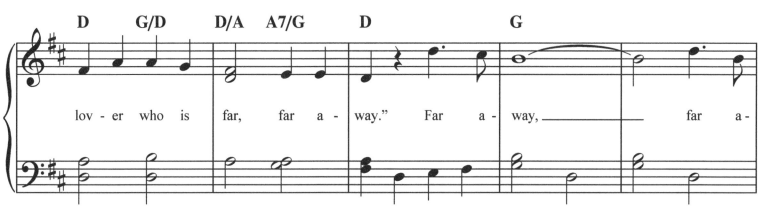

lov - er who is far, far a - way." Far a - way, _____ far a-

way. _____ She wore it for her lov - er far a - way. _____

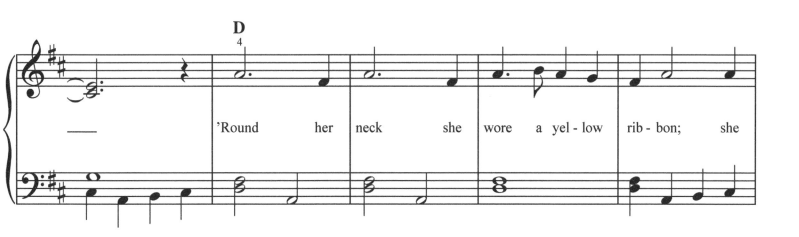

_____ 'Round her neck she wore a yel - low rib - bon; she

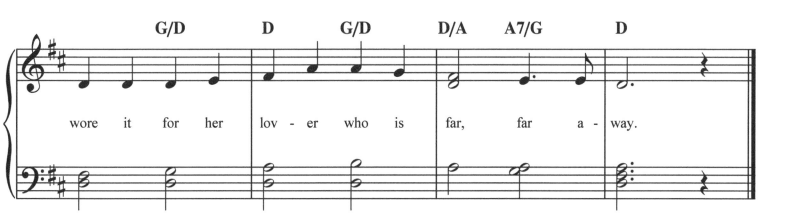

wore it for her lov - er who is far, far a - way.

SOMETIMES I FEEL LIKE A MOTHERLESS CHILD

African-American Spiritual

THERE IS A TAVERN IN THE TOWN

Traditional Drinking Song

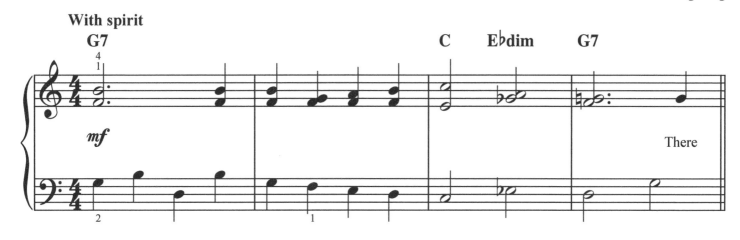

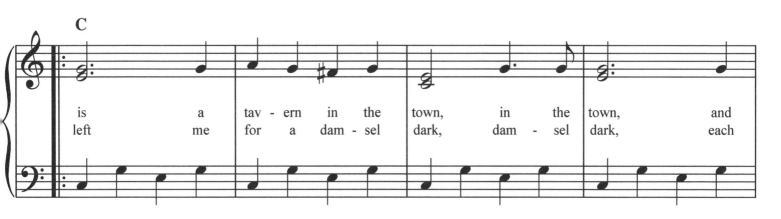

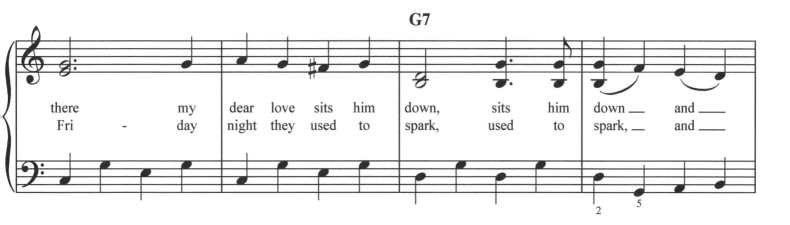

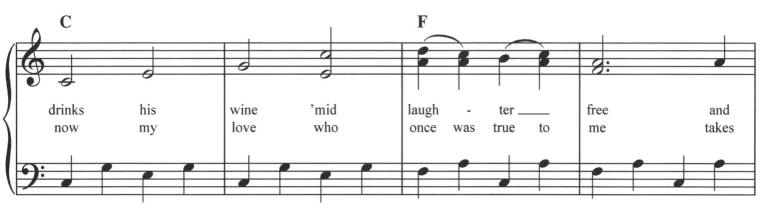

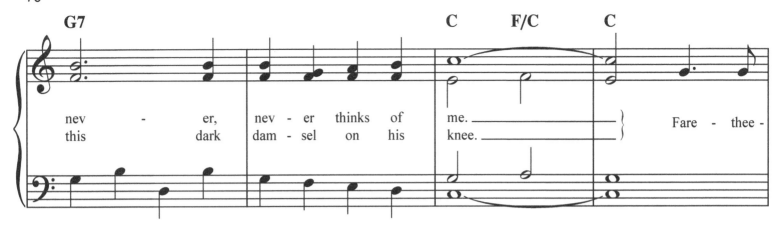

nev - er, nev - er thinks of me. _____ Fare - thee -
this dark dam - sel on his knee. _____

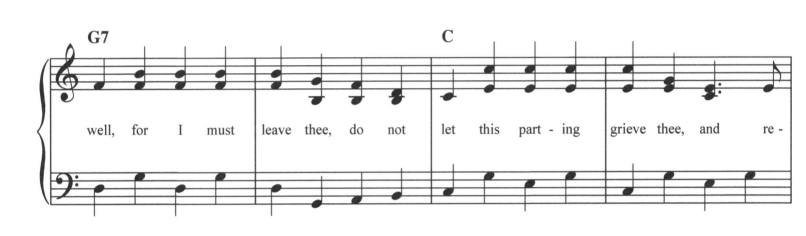

well, for I must leave thee, do not let this part - ing grieve thee, and re -

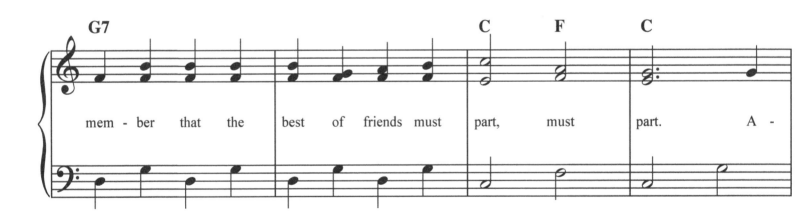

mem - ber that the best of friends must part, must part. A -

dieu, a - dieu, kind friends, a - dieu, a - dieu, a - dieu, I

can   no   long - er   stay   with   you,   stay   with   you, ___   I'll ___

hang   my   heart   on   a   weep - ing   wil - low

tree,   and   may   the   world   go   well   with

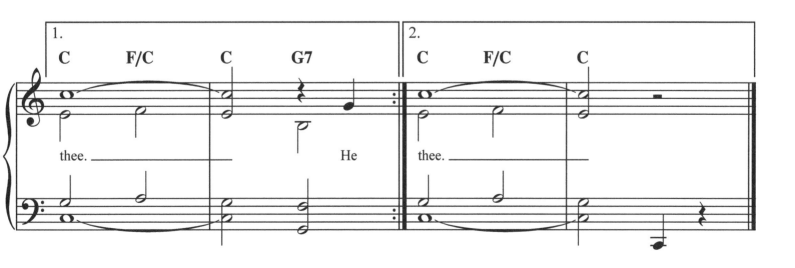

thee. _____   He   thee. _____

THIS LITTLE LIGHT OF MINE

African-American Spiritual

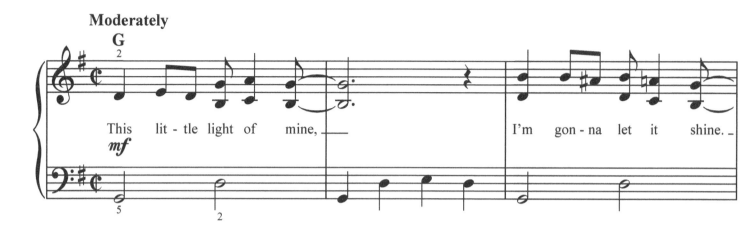

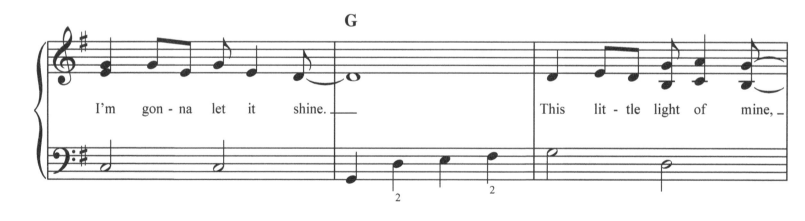

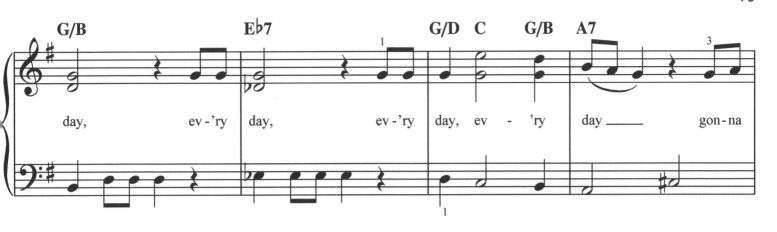

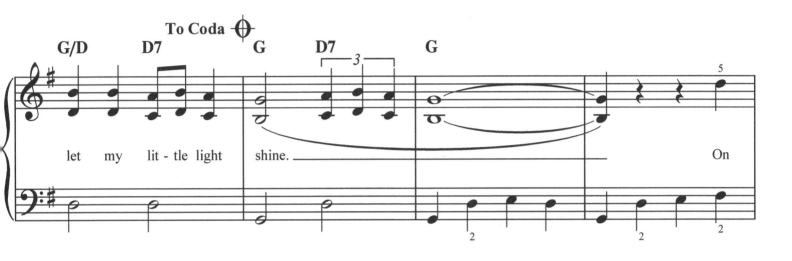

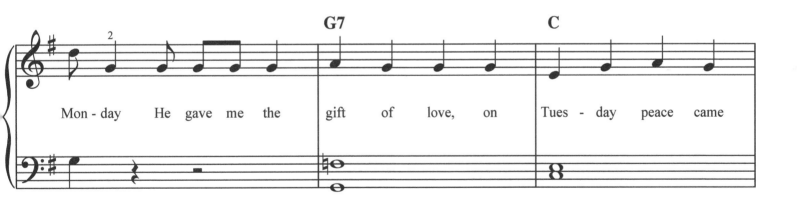

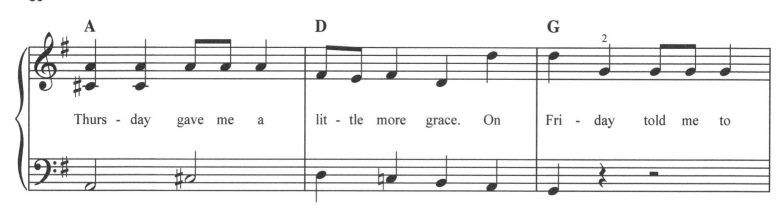

Thurs - day gave me a lit - tle more grace. On Fri - day told me to

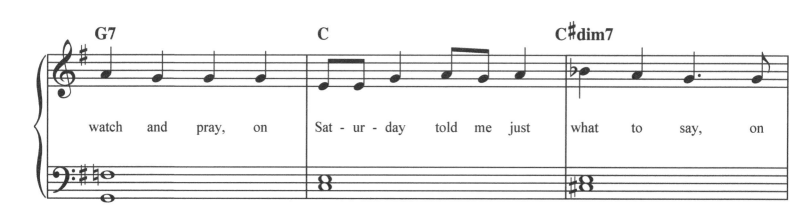

watch and pray, on Sat - ur - day told me just what to say, on

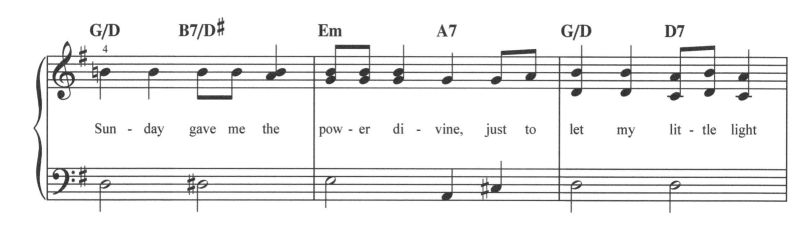

Sun - day gave me the pow - er di - vine, just to let my lit - tle light

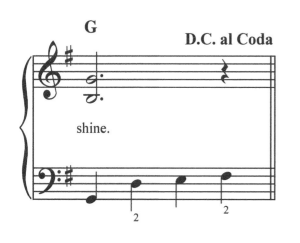

shine.

D.C. al Coda

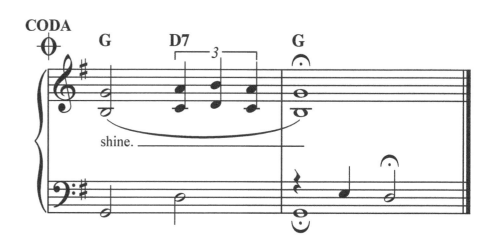

CODA

shine.

THE WABASH CANNON BALL

Hobo Song

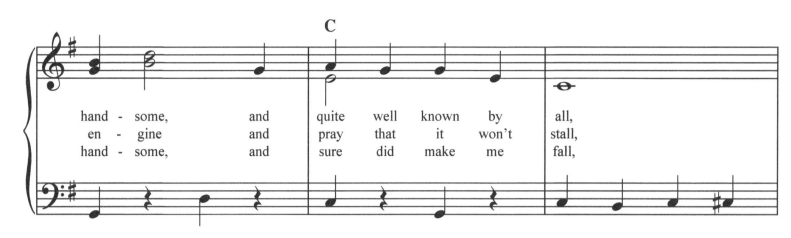

hand - some,   and   quite   well   known   by   all,
en - gine   and   pray   that   it   won't   stall,
hand - some,   and   sure   did   make   me   fall,

how   we   love   the   choo   choo   of   the   Wa - bash   Can - non -
while   we   safe - ly   trav - el   on   the   Wa - bash   Can - non -
he's   a - com - ing   toward   me   on   the   Wa - bash   Can - non -

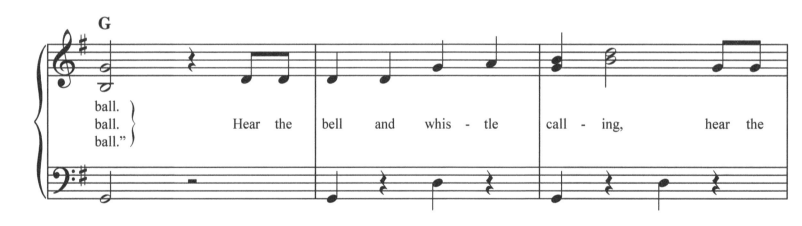

ball.
ball.   Hear   the   bell   and   whis - tle   call - ing,   hear   the
ball."

wheels   that   go   "clack   clack,"   hear   the   roar - ing   of   the

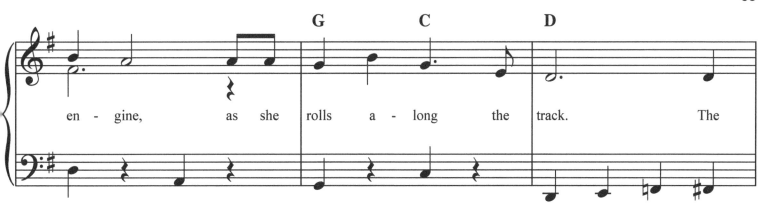

en - gine, as she rolls a - long the track. The

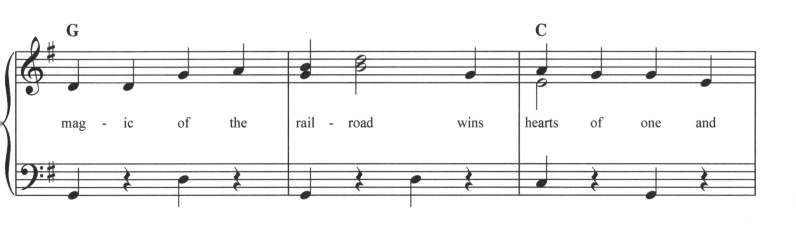

mag - ic of the rail - road wins hearts of one and

all, as we reach our des - tin - a - tion on the

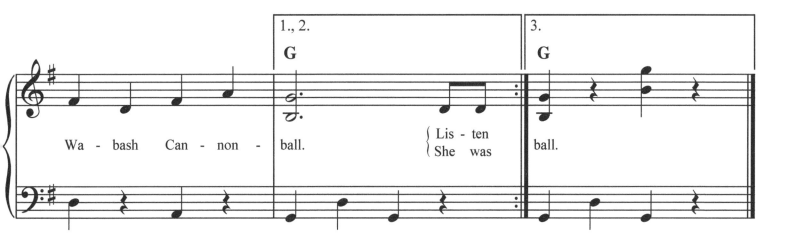

Wa - bash Can - non - ball.

1., 2.
Lis - ten
She was

3.
ball.

THIS TRAIN

Traditional

With spirit

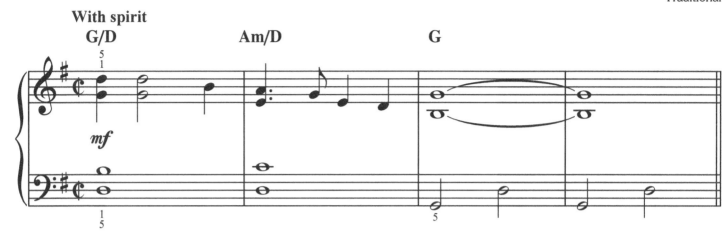

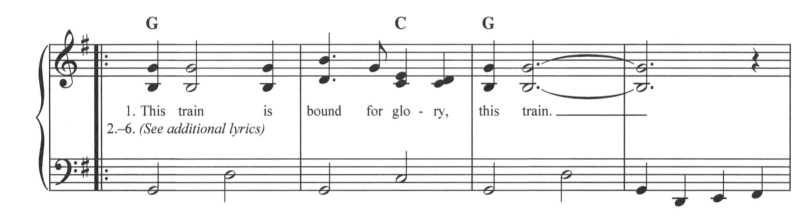

1. This train is bound for glo-ry, this train.___
2.–6. *(See additional lyrics)*

This train is bound for glo-ry, this train.

This train is bound for glo-ry, don't ride noth-in' but the

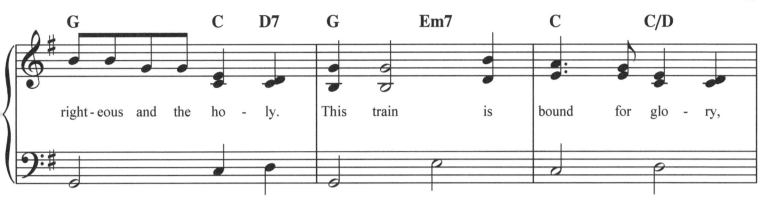

Additional Lyrics

2. This train don't carry no gamblers, this train. (2 times)
   This train don't carry no gamblers,
   No hypocrites, no midnight ramblers.
   This train is bound for glory, this train.

3. This train is built for speed now, this train. (2 times)
   This train is built for speed now,
   Fastest train you ever did see.
   This train is bound for glory, this train.

4. This train don't carry no liars, this train. (2 times)
   This train don't carry no liars,
   No hypocrites and no high flyers.
   This train is bound for glory, this train.

5. This train you don't pay no transportation, this train. (2 times)
   This train you don't pay no transportation,
   No Jim Crow and no discrimination.
   This train is bound for glory, this train.

6. This train don't carry no rustlers, this train. (2 times)
   This train don't carry no rustlers,
   Sidestreet walkers, two-bit hustlers.
   This train is bound for glory, this train.

TURKEY IN THE STRAW

American Folksong

Bright Hoedown tempo

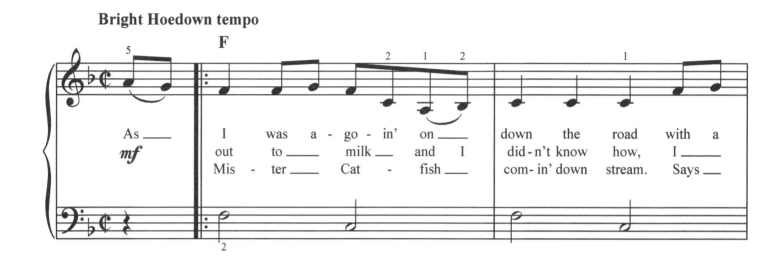

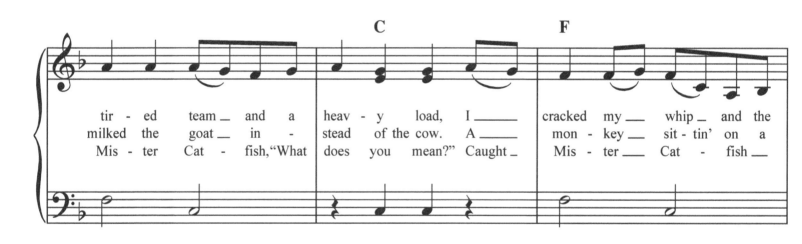

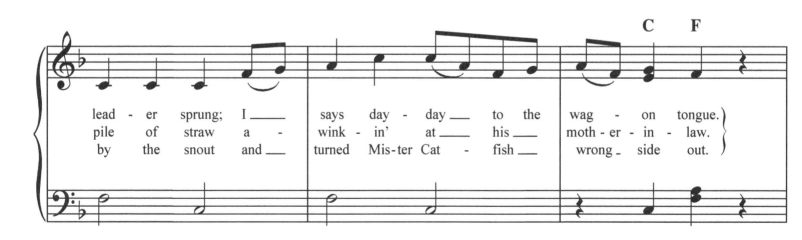

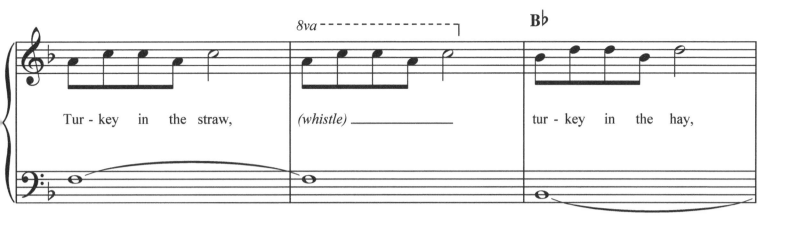

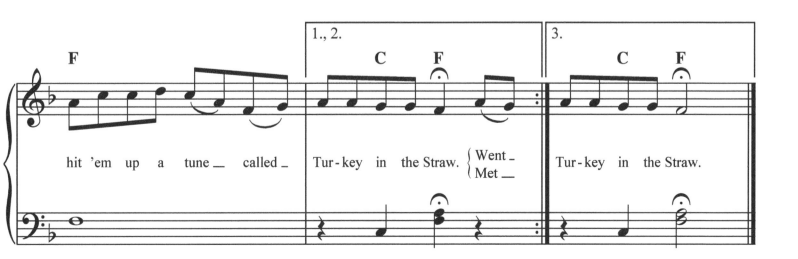

WATER IS WIDE

Traditional

Moderately slow

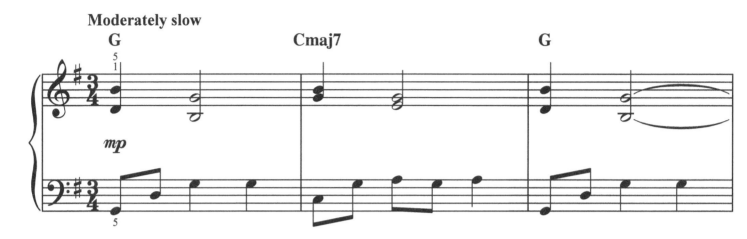

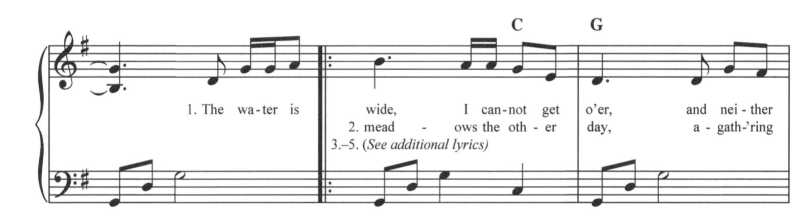

1. The wa-ter is wide, I can-not get o'er, and nei-ther
2. mead - ows the oth - er day, a - gath-'ring
3.–5. (*See additional lyrics*)

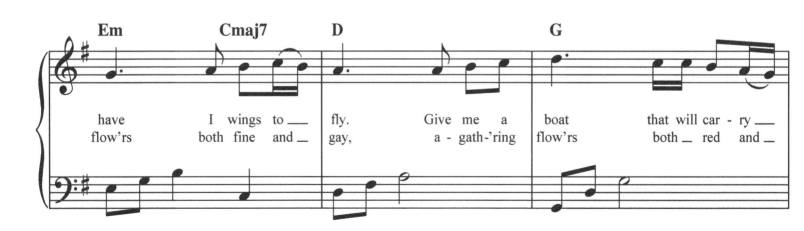

have I wings to ___ fly. Give me a boat that will car - ry
flow'rs both fine and ___ gay, a - gath-'ring flow'rs both ___ red and ___

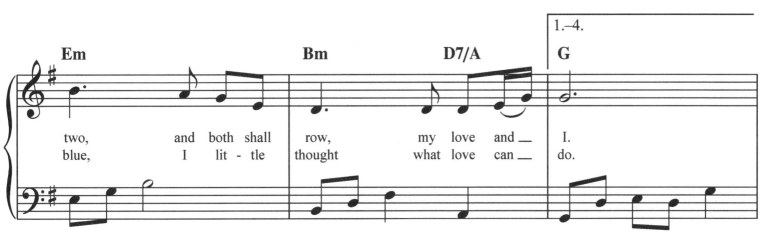

Additional Lyrics

3. I leaned my back up against some oak
   Thinking that she was a trusty tree;
   But first she bended and then she broke;
   And so did my false love to me.

4. A ship there is, and she sails the sea,
   She's loaded deep as deep can be,
   But not so deep as the love I'm in:
   I know not if I sink or swim.

5. Oh, love is handsome and love is fine,
   And love's a jewel while it is new;
   But when it is old, it groweth cold,
   And fades away like morning dew.

WHEN JOHNNY COMES MARCHING HOME

Words and Music by
PATRICK SARSFIELD GILMORE

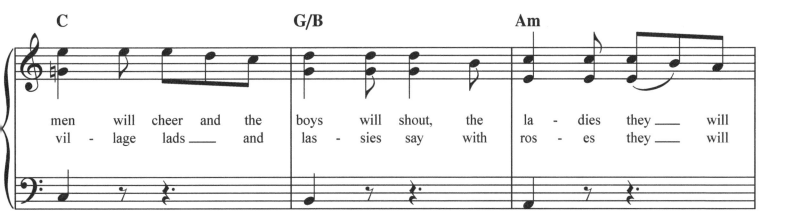

men will cheer and the boys will shout, the la - dies they ___ will
vil - lage lads ___ and las - sies say with ros - es they ___ will

all turn out, and we'll shout hoo - ray when
strew the way, and we'll shout hoo - ray when

John - ny comes march - ing home. The
John - ny comes march - ing home.

WHEN THE SAINTS GO MARCHING IN

Words by KATHERINE E. PURVIS
Music by JAMES M. BLACK

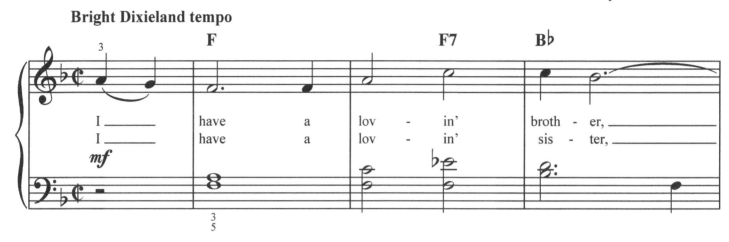

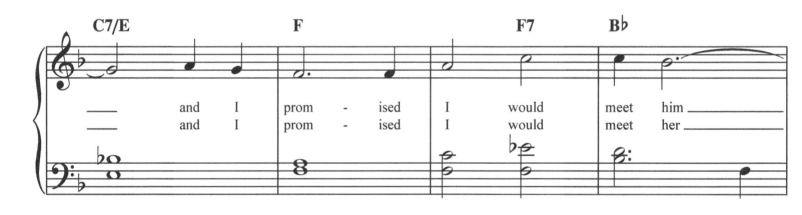

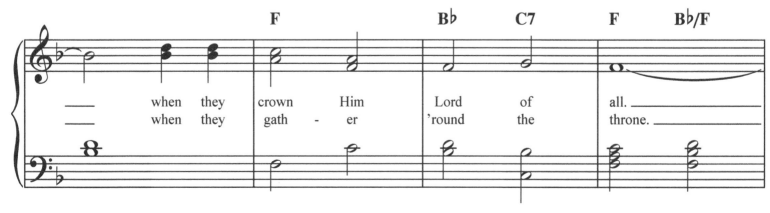

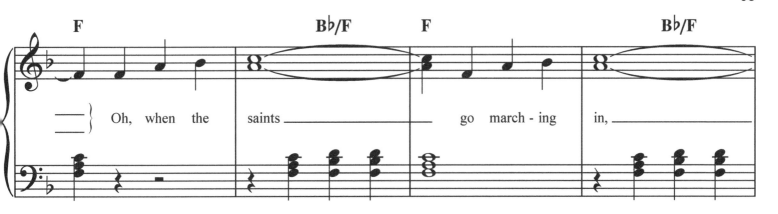

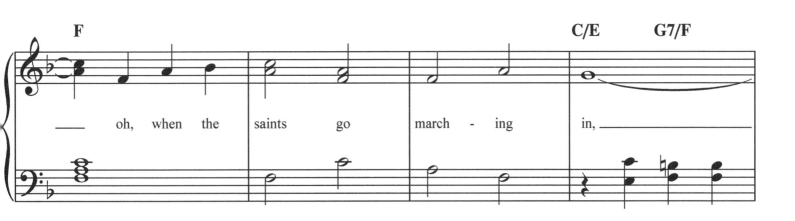

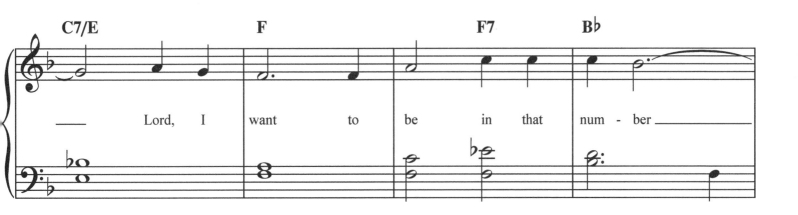

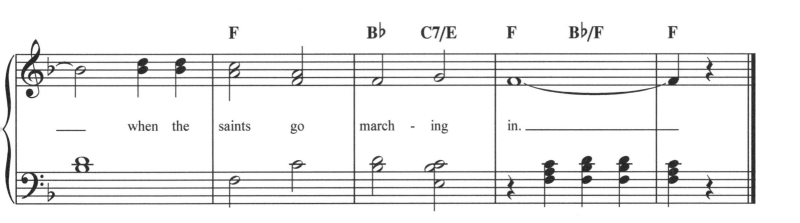

WILDWOOD FLOWER

Traditional

I'll en-

twine	and	I'll	min	-	gle	my	ra	-	ven	black
prom	-	ised	to	love		me,	he	called		me	his
dance	and	to	sing,		and	my	heart		will	be

hair	with	the	ros	-	es	so	red	and	the
flower.	He	said	I	was	the	blos	-	som	to
gay.	No	more	tears,	no	more	sighs,	no	to	more

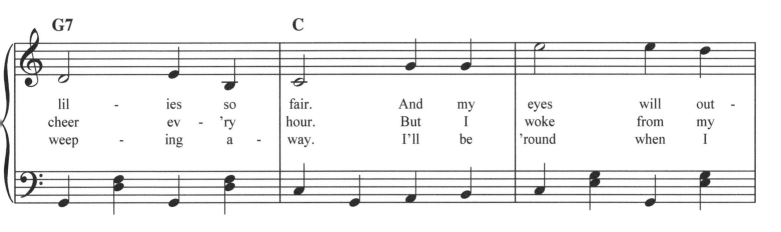

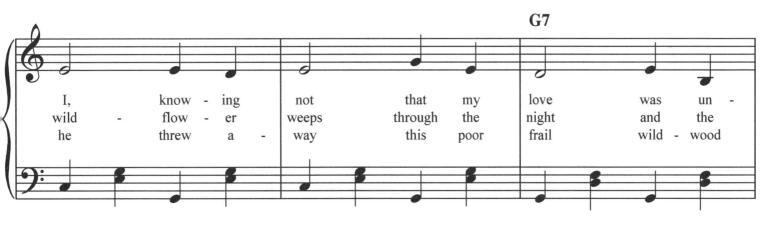

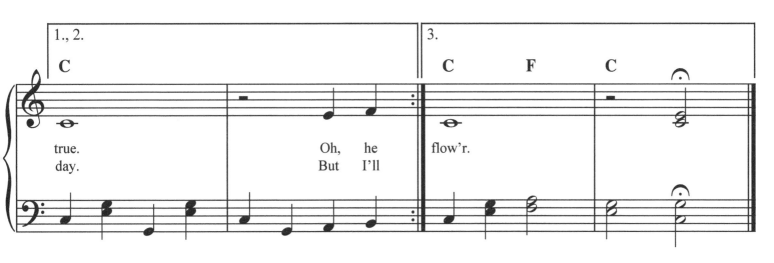

WORRIED MAN BLUES

Traditional

Moderately

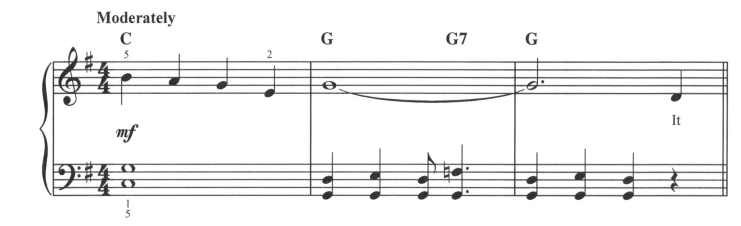

It

takes a wor- ried man to sing a wor- ried
ev - 'ry- thing goes wrong, I sing a wor- ried
saved a thou- sand bucks, then I met Jen - nie
has its ups and downs, I'm down more than I'm

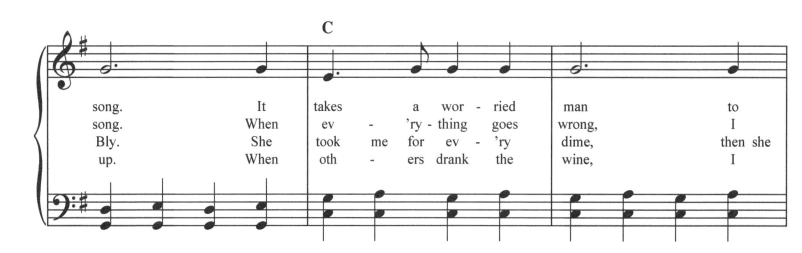

song. It takes a wor - ried man to
song. When ev - 'ry- thing goes wrong, I
Bly. She took me for ev - 'ry dime, then she
up. When oth - ers drank the wine, I

YANKEE DOODLE

Traditional

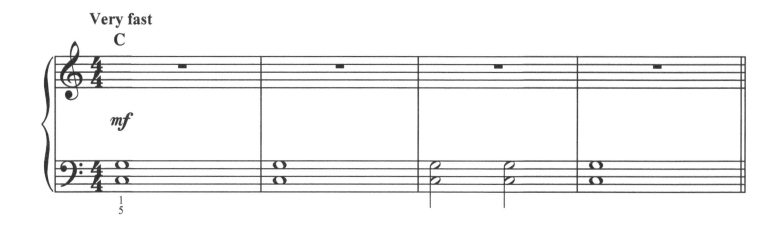

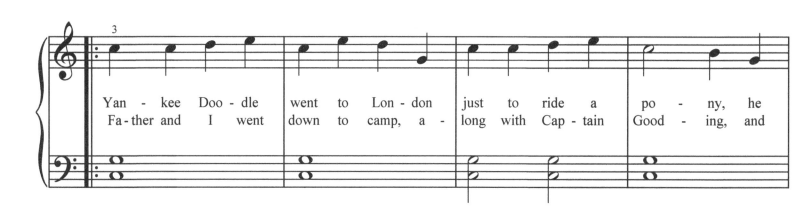

Yan - kee Doo - dle went to Lon - don just to ride a po - ny, he
Fa - ther and I went down to camp, a - long with Cap - tain Good - ing, and

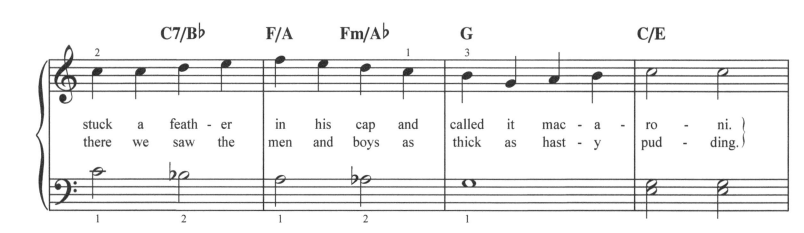

C7/B♭   F/A   Fm/A♭   G   C/E

stuck a feath - er in his cap and called it mac - a - ro - ni.
there we saw the men and boys as thick as hast - y pud - ding.

Yan - kee Doo - dle, keep it up, Yan - kee Doo - dle dan - dy.

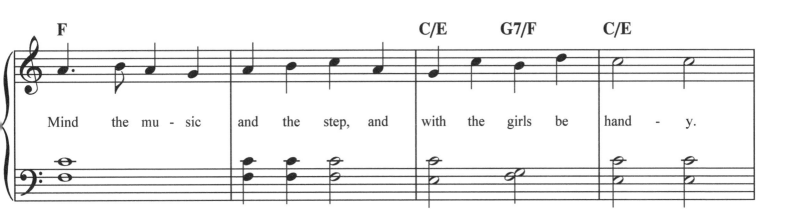

Mind the mu - sic and the step, and with the girls be hand - y.

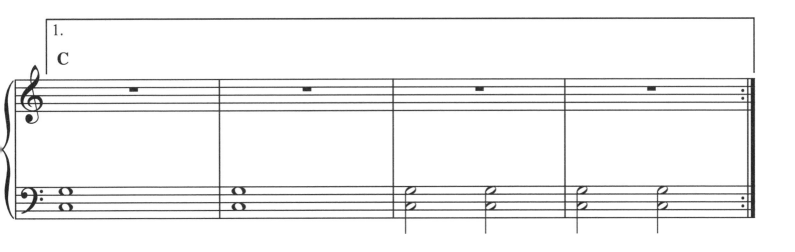

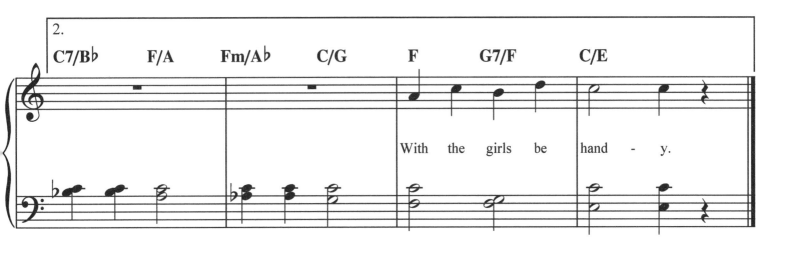

With the girls be hand - y.

THE YELLOW ROSE OF TEXAS

Words and Music by
J.K., 1858

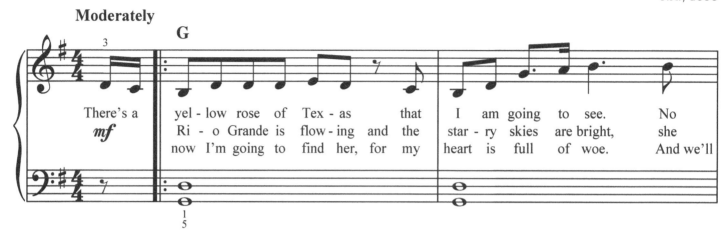

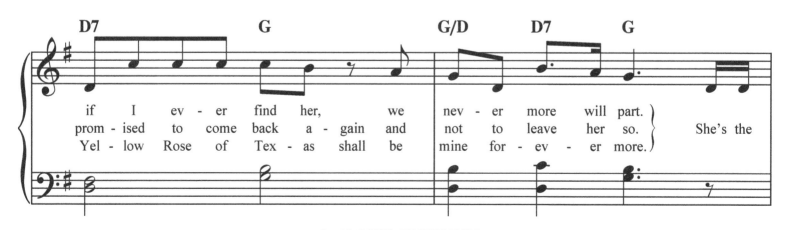

sweet-est rose of col - or this fel - low ev - er knew. Her eyes are bright as dia-monds; they

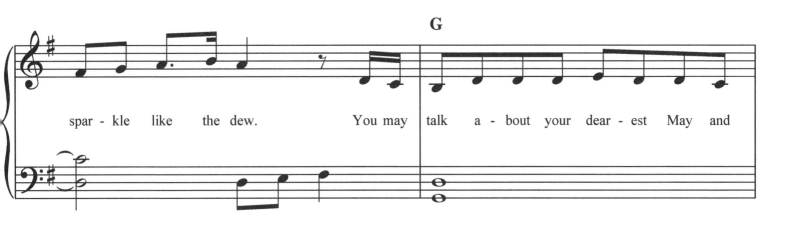

spar - kle like the dew. You may talk a - bout your dear - est May and

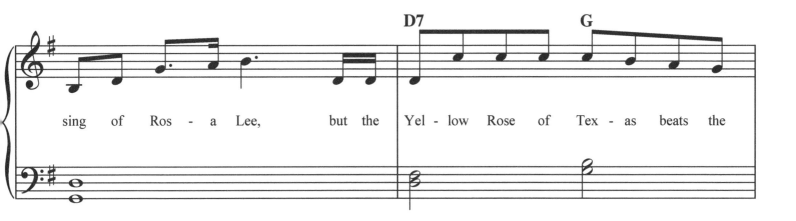

sing of Ros - a Lee, but the Yel - low Rose of Tex - as beats the

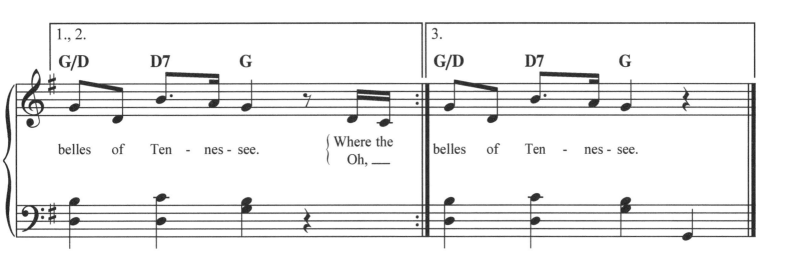

belles of Ten - nes - see. { Where the / Oh, ___ } belles of Ten - nes - see.

WILL THE CIRCLE BE UNBROKEN

Words by ADA R. HABERSHON
Music by CHARLES H. GABRIEL

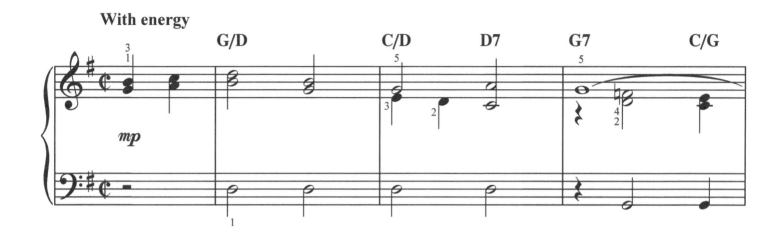

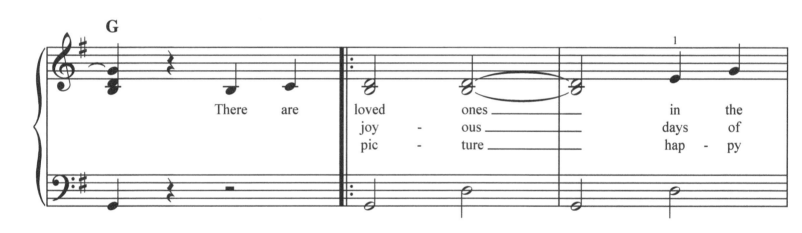

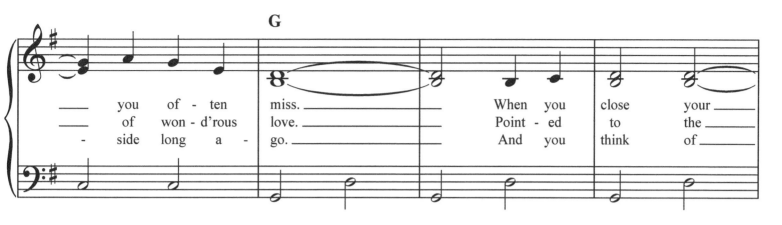

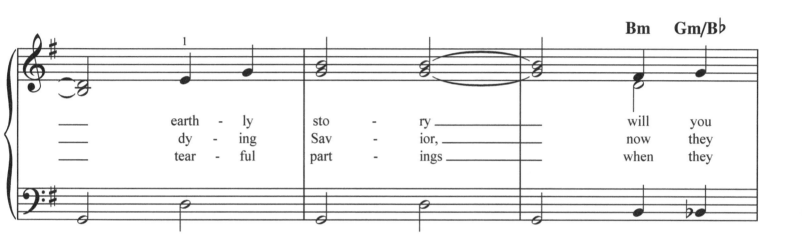

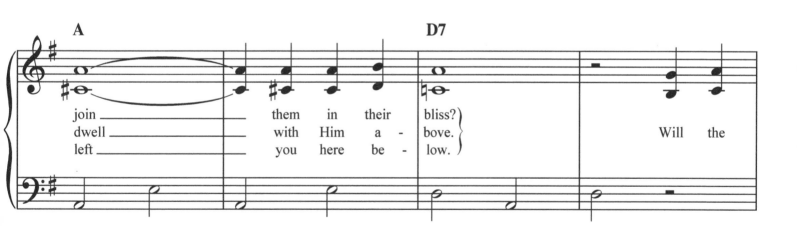

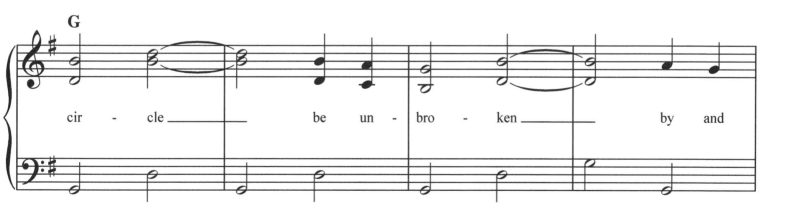

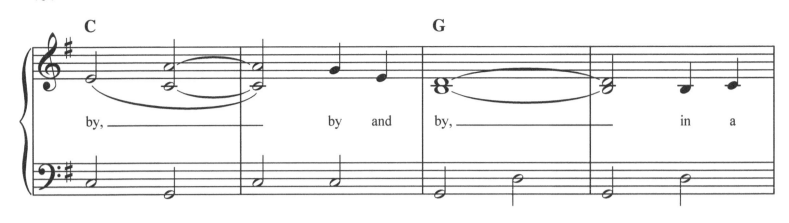

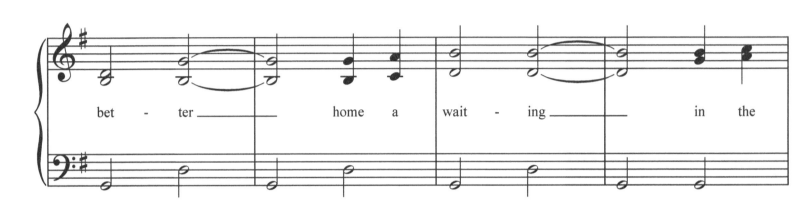

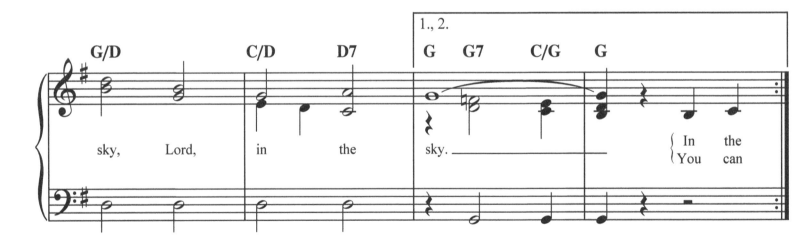